FUN ON SKATES!

If there is such a thing as a universal sport for everybody, surely it must be roller skating. You will see two-year-olds whizzing along on these wheeled shoes. At the other end of the life span, there was a man out in Ohio who did not throw his skates back in the closet until he was ninety. Now it is pretty hard to find that age range in any other sport.

And as for those who think skating is just something kids do on sidewalks, they haven't been keeping up with the times—the *good times,* as today's mod skater will tell you.

There does not seem to be anything that one cannot do on skates these days—and this book will show you how to get the most fun out of this popular sport!

I.G. EDMONDS

ROLLER SKATING
A Beginner's Guide

ILLUSTRATED WITH PHOTOGRAPHS AND DIAGRAMS

PUBLISHED BY POCKET BOOKS NEW YORK

Another *Original* publication of POCKET BOOKS

POCKET BOOKS, a Simon & Schuster division of
GULF & WESTERN CORPORATION
1230 Avenue of the Americas, New York, N.Y. 10020

ISBN: 0-671-56015-8

First Pocket Books printing August, 1979

10 9 8 7 6 5 4 3 2 1

Trademarks registered in the United States and other countries.

Printed in the U.S.A.

To Annette and Cary

Contents

CHAPTER 1

ROLLING ALONG

If there is such a thing as a universal sport for everybody, surely it must be roller skating. You will see two-year-olds whizzing along on these wheeled shoes. At the other end of the life span, there was a man out in Ohio who did not throw his skates back in the closet until he was ninety. Now it is pretty hard to find that age range in any other sport.

And as for those who think skating is just something kids do on sidewalks, they haven't been keeping up with the times—the *good times,* as today's mod skaters will tell you.

There does not seem to be anything that one cannot do on skates these days. For starters, you can use skates to move up and down the road faster and easier than you can walk.

From this modest beginning, you can branch out into fantastic roller-skating activities. You can race on your wheels, becoming a speed champion. If you are the playful type, there

1

This is roller skating—just swinging along enjoying yourself. . . .

are all kinds of games you can play on skates. These might be roller polo, roller basketball, roller touch football, or even roller tennis. The skating tennis players I once saw did not do too well, I'll admit.

If you are a really hardy soul and think getting hit over the head with a stick is great fun, then you might think about going in for roller hockey. This sport is very popular in the northeastern part of the country. It is well to re-

But taking the baby for a stroll can also be roller skating . . .

Or if you feel like jumping over a line of trash cans, it is another way to enjoy roller skating . . .

And here is still another form of roller skating. Having reached the peak in a dramatic climb in a skate park concrete "pipe," the skater is on his way down. Skating is never dull. There is something in it for every taste.

member that hockey players, be it field, ice or roller, are a tough bunch of men, and you had better be tough yourself.

On With the Dance

Feel like dancing? Don't bother to take off your skates. Fred Astaire, the dancing whiz, did a wonderful dance on skates in one of his early films. That started a craze for skate dancing that became a national fad. And it is still going on. Recently I observed a young man roll over on his ankles, pop back up again and kick his heels like a chorus girl from Las Vegas. Then he did a bump and grind, along with a twist this way and that. He was no John Travolta, but for disco dancing *on skates* he was pretty good. Roller-skate dancing has kept up with the passing years.

Or you might want to get into roller figure skating. You can cut Figure 8s and do just about anything else an ice skater can do. Also, if you fall, it is not as cold. As a matter of fact, it was an ice skater who is supposed to have invented roller skates.

This genius, to whom we should all give a deep bow of thankfulness, was a Hans Brinker type who loved ice skating. When spring brought an end to skating on the canals in his native Holland, he fashioned wheels for his ice skates. The legend says that the wheels were enlarged wooden spools. Apparently, they did not work too well, for no one made wheeled ice skates a booming fad. Then later improvements developed a true roller skate and roller skaters began copying ice-skating techniques to give birth to figure roller skating.

Other Skating Tricks

You can catch frisbees on roller skates. There are roller skating exhibition tricks, like jumping over a line of barrels or looping-the-loop in the concrete tracks at the new skateboard parks. Skating rinks sponsor all kinds of competitions. Some of these are purely local and some are sponsored nationally through the Roller Skating Rink Operators Association's sanctions.

You might also get into Roller Derbies. They are really exciting, and also tough going—although not as dangerous as roller hockey sometimes gets. Or if you really like to get around, you can pull on your skates and take off across the country. Several people over the years have skated from coast to coast. In 1933 a woman—Gerane Withington—did it the hard way. She skated a diagonal cross-country course from Oregon to Florida.

You can skate alone, or you can join a club. You can take the sidewalk—unless local laws forbid it—or you can go to a skating rink. Some parks and recreation areas have special roller-skating paths laid out.

If lonesome, you might even do some court-ing on skates. This seems to be what happened to Randy Dayney, a former world champion figure roller skater. Randy went to Europe for an international competition. There he met Pe-tra Hausler, a young German girl who twice won the women's world title for figure and freestyle figure skating. Now the two have a lifetime partnership, and it was roller skates that played Cupid for them.

And just to prove that you can do just about anything on skates, here is an extreme exam-ple. I once knew a boy who went swimming in skates. I'll admit that he did not intend to do it. He rolled off a pier while trying to show off to impress some young girls who were watch-ing him.

It's Really Easy

The things one can do on skates seem end-less. However, since this is a guide for begin-ners, we will not be able to go into the more complicated forms of skating. We may touch on some in passing, but cannot go into them too deeply. For one thing, it is dangerous to attempt exhibition jumping without an instruc-tor to guide you. Disco dancing is another complicated routine. Here you had best learn to give the Travolta shake on a regular disco dancefloor and then move into skates.

However, basic skating is not difficult to

learn. In a very short time you should be moving along well enough to begin adding the simpler trick maneuvers to your routine.

The most important thing to learn is *balance*. Once you can balance yourself correctly on moving skates, the battle is really won. You have only to learn the basic movements for different routines and you are on your way.

The basic movements that you must learn are:

- STARTING. This is how to get moving from a dead stop. You must be smooth and graceful. This is essential if you want to continue in competition where grace means the difference between winning and losing.
- STOPPING. This is as important as starting. It is more difficult to do correctly than starting.
- FORWARD MOVEMENT. Moving forward is not skating in a straight line. That would simply be walking on skates. You swing along with slightly sideways curves that add together to make you go forward.
- RIGHT AND LEFT CURVES. You curve your skate path the same way a motorcyclist turns his cycle. You *lean* in the direction of the turn, creating what skaters call an *edge*. This is easily learned. The entire secret of a good turn is in the way you hold your body. This works in con-

The proper lean of your body causes your skates to make a curving turn.

    junction with balance to gracefully curve you around.

These four steps or movements—starting, stopping, going forward and curving right and left—are all you need to know to become a good skater. There are two other movements, spins and jumps, but they are specialized and we will not go into them. You need expert coaching when you try jumps and spins.

Except for routines involving spins, jumps and backward skating—none of which a person in the beginner's rank should try anyway— every maneuver in roller skating is just a combination of these simple steps: starting, stopping, going forward and making circles and turns. Everything from speed racing on skates to waltzing and disco dancing are made up of these basic movements.

It Takes Practice

While you only have these basic maneuvers to learn, when you start putting the elements together the situation can get tricky at times. In some routines, you may need to shift from foot to foot. In others you must start with sufficient speed to carry you through two complete circles. In another you may be required to reverse yourself, turning and skating backward.

None of these is difficult to do, but they do require practice and lots of it, if you want to be really good. If you only want to skate for fun, then you don't have to work so hard at constant practice.

Unfortunately for the lazy among us, we don't always skate alone. This is especially true if we join a skating club or skate at a roller

The principles of skating are simple and easy to learn. After that, it is a matter of lots of practice before you are doing fast spins like this skater.

rink. The fun we get from sloppy skating goes sour when some clever boy or girl slips past us as smoothly as a happy dream. We would like to do that, too. A better pair of skates might help us some. A good teacher can point out the right direction for us to follow, but the real payoff in becoming a good skater comes only through hard, long and sincere practice on roller skates. You can't get anywhere unless you roll. After all, skating is fun and that is why we do it. Practice should be enjoyable and no problem at all. Sadly enough, it does not work out quite this way. Skaters get bored going over and over the same movement. They want to get rolling. This is understandable, but look at it this way: If you want to win competitions, it is not enough to just be good. You must be the *best*.

How to Be the Best

You get to be the best by thoroughly learning each of the four basic movements. Then you expand by adding just a little more.

Okay, you can now skate in a straight line without falling down. Then you learn to lean properly to make a curve. When you can easily make a right and left turn, you continue this turn until you can make a circle. This circle must be a smooth, graceful glide that produces a full turn and not a lopsided, shaky goose egg.

When you can make a good circle, you are ready for your first figure. This is a basic routine in figure skating. It is the well-known Figure 8 (also called Circle 8). It is simply skating two circles. Draw two circles on the rink floor. Let them touch at one point. Place your right skate on the point where the circles touch. The left foot is behind to push off with. Now skate clockwise up the edge of the top circle. Curve right on around and come back to the point where you started, at the point where the circles touch. Don't stop, switch to your left foot and skate counterclockwise around the lower circle, coming back to the original starting point where the two circles touch each other.

You have now made a complete Figure 8 (Circle 8), one of the compulsory figures you must make in figure skating competitions. These are known as "compulsory school figures."

To make this Figure 8, all you did was start and move ahead in one continuous turn to the right. When you completed the top circle, you changed to the left foot and made the second circle in one continuous left turn. There is nothing new that you did not learn in your basic maneuvers.

Sounds simple? It is simple—if you learn each step thoroughly as you go ahead.

Adding Something New

Now let's consider a more complicated figure—the Serpentine. This is a graceful weaving routine when viewed from the audience. But

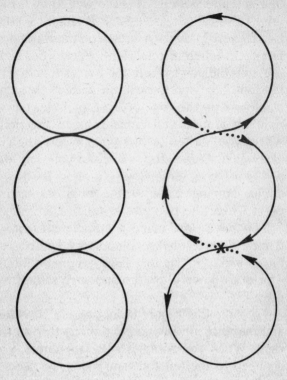

In skating the three-circle Serpentine, the three touching circles at left will be the pattern drawn on the rink floor. The three circles at right show how you skate the pattern. The dotted lines show where the skating path crosses another line. You begin skating at X where the bottom and middle circles touch.

from the skater's position it is just the old Figure 8 done with three circles instead of two.

The three-circle pattern is drawn on the rink floor. The circles are in line and each touches the adjacent one at one point. Start exactly as you did for the Figure 8—that is, at the point where the lower two circles touch each other. Skate to the right, following the line (trace) of the right circle. Then, instead of looping this (now the middle) circle, you change feet at the point where this middle circle touches the top circle and circle it completely. Then you retrace the other half of the middle circle and the entire lower circle to return to your starting point; that is, where the lower two circles touch each other.

This is little different from the Figure 8, and the difference is only in the directions in which the turns are made and not in any basically new actions. In other words, it is just the same as before, except that we have added one more step.

In the same manner, the basic Figure 8 can be turned into other school figures by slight additions.

Later we will go into these school figures more deeply. They are only mentioned here to illustrate with a brief sketch the basic simplicity of what looks difficult when viewed from the audience.

School figures, incidentally, are supposed to include most of the movements of skating. So

Very small children fall often while learning to skate. But they are rarely hurt because they do not have far to fall. This is especially true when they have well-padded behinds to plop down on and wear protectors to avoid scraped knees.

practicing them gives you an almost total workout.

Who Can Skate?

Practically anyone who has enough sense of balance to stand up and walk can learn to skate. While there have been skaters—and pretty good ones—as young as two years old, instructors usually recommend starting around age four. If you are really serious about competition skating, the younger you start the better.

Actually there seems to be less danger of getting hurt on skates at an early age than when one is older. Yes, you can break bones, get skinned up, and even get killed. But you can do that just by walking down the street and tripping yourself. I believe that those who keep statistics on such things claim the home is actually the source of more accidents than any other place.

Skaters come in all sizes and ages. The younger you start, the better.

Jumping requires a stronger body than some other types of skating.

Skating accidents can be minimized by proper attention to safety rules. We will go into that very thoroughly in another chapter.

How far you can go in competition skating and how well you can do in any kind of fun skating depends a lot on the type of body you have. A husky football center will not make it in roller acrobatics, for example. This takes a lighter, younger frame. We have seen a classic example of this in the last Olympics. Tiny Nadia Comaneci swept through the gymnastics with perfect scores. But two years later, having grown and filled out, this Olympic star lost out to a younger Russian team in the European games. She had simply outgrown this type of competition.

On the other hand, the light, supple skater who would be so good at doing roller acrobatics would possibly lack the strength to do some of the more complicated dance routines that require lifting his partner—unless the partner were very small.

The husky type, on the other hand, is just what the coach is praying for when he sets up a roller hockey team. He wants someone the opposing team cannot run over.

So there is a place for you in skating, either in competition or just rolling along for the sheer joy of it. Don't worry about what that place is at first. As you learn to skate, you will gradually find the place nature intended for you.

CHAPTER 2

WHAT ARE SKATES?

The first question a beginner seeks an answer to in a book or from an instructor is generally, "How do I get rolling?"

Well, shoving off on your first roll on wheeled shoes is a basic part of learning to skate. However, it is a long way from being the first step. There are many very important things to learn and do before you make your first roll. There are such questions to answer as what skates to buy, how to put them on, how to take care of them, how to balance yourself so you can stand up and how to take care of yourself when you fall. Now notice that we said *when* you fall, not *if* you fall. I don't care who you are, you are going to take your share of bounces off the concrete or rink floor. Or if you do manage to get along without an occasional sprawl, you will be a candidate for having a statue raised to you. You will have done something no other skater in history has accomplished. But don't

let the thought of a few bounces worry you.
There are ways to soften them up. We'll go
into that in the chapter on safety.

This Is a Skate

Perhaps your very first question should be,
"What is a skate anyway?"

Maybe you know. A lot of beginners do not.
They may think they know. They may say,
"Skates are wheels you tie on your feet so you
can roll instead of walk."

And that is right as far as it goes. In fact,
that is all a nonskater needs to know. But skaters need to know about such things as plates,
pivots, trucks, cushions, kinds of wheels, toe
stops and different types of boots. Unless you
know about these things, you do not know
what a pair of roller skates really is.

Old Skates and New

Skates have changed a lot in the last few
years. But the change has not been so great
that the legendary Dutchman who started it all
could not recognize what he created when he
put wooden rollers on his ice skates back in
seventeenth century Holland.

The Dutchman's idea did not catch on then.
It took another hundred years before skating
was back in the news—and it proved to be a
sad tale indeed. In 1760 a Belgian inventor was
showing off his metal-wheeled roller skates at

a party in London. He had evidently worked up an exhibition act in which he played a violin as he skated.

He only had two wheels on each skate instead of the four we have today. They were in line. This did not permit him to make turns. He did not know how to stop, either. Things went well as long as he glided back and forth at a slow speed. Then the audience's applause spurred him to increase his efforts. This was disastrous. He was unable to stop. A report of this sad affair said, "He impelled himself against a large mirror, dashing it to bits, smashing his violin to pieces, and wounding himself most severely."

From his experience we can draw a modern lesson applicable to all wheeled sports: "Before you learn to *start,* for goodness sake learn to *stop.*"

After this sad situation we do not hear anymore about roller skating until 1790 when it reappeared in Paris. Skating still did not catch on. The problem of turning had not yet been solved. There was novelty in skimming along in a straight line, hobbling around and coming back, but it soon got boring.

Skating Goes Up in the Aria

Then something happened that aroused the public fancy. Skating literally became the "grand opera" of sport. In 1849 the Paris Opera House staged a new opera called *Le Pro-phete*. It called for an ice-skating scene wherein the prima donna gave out with her aria while gracefully gliding along with the chorus.

There was no way to make an artificial ice rink then as we would do now. Some technical genius in the opera's property shop came up with the idea of roller skates. These were specially built. Those for the male members of the cast were made with two wheels in a straight line. The ones for the ladies of the chorus were made like today's skates with four wheels. One pair was in front. The second pair was in the back. Both were on a plate that clamped to the wearers' shoe soles.

The opera was a smash success. The "ice-skating" scene drew raves from the audiences. Immediately a company rushed out copies of the skates, which it called "Prophete skates." Skating became a fad that spread across the channel to England.

Plimpton's "Rocking Skate"

After this, "off-ice skating," as it was called, became increasingly popular. But it was a gentleman from Massachusetts whom we can thank for finally getting the big rolling show on the road. He was James Plimpton who patented his "rocking skate" in 1863.

Plimpton earned his title of "father of roller skating" by inventing a way to gracefully curve rolling skates. Before this the only way to turn the solidly fixed wheels was either to stop and hop around or jump in the air and try to twist around before gravity got you back on the ground.

Plimpton used a metal plate that fitted under the sole of the shoe. Four wheels were attached to this. Two wheels were placed under the ball of the wearer's foot. The other two were placed under the heel.

The wheels were arranged so that if the skater leaned to one side, it would cause the two outside wheels on the leaning side to move closer together. The wheels on the outside of the lean would move slightly farther apart. This caused the moving skate to turn in the direction of lean.

This is exactly the same situation we have when we turn on modern skates, although there have been improvements since "Father" Plimpton got skaters going around in circles.

Plimpton called his invention "rocking skates" because the lean rocked the wheels into position to make them pull to the right or left.

This ability to move roller skates along a curved line made it possible for the sport to expand into routines approaching those of ice skating. It had taken about 200 years but the old Dutchman's dream of "ice skating" in the summer had finally come true.

Since then roller skating has had its booms

and recessions. But it has always come back more popular than ever.

Kinds of Skates

There are several kinds of skates, but they all break down into two definite types. One is the standard or clamp skate. The other is the shoe or boot skate.

The standard skate is the old standby. It has a metal plate to the underside of which the wheels and trucks are attached. You place your shoe sole on the top side. A strap in the back fits around your ankle. The toe of your shoe is held to the plate by two adjustable clamps that grasp the shoe sole. A key on the bottom lets you tighten the clamps to hold your shoe.

PLATE

PLATE

ADJUSTING NUT
CUSHIONS

TOE STOP

POLYURETHANE WHEEL

This shows the major parts of a boot skate.

The shoe or boot skate is made in one unit. The plate is permanently fastened to the boot sole. You buy these skates as a unit or you can have the plate attached to your own boots. These skates are more expensive than the standard skate. But if you do much roller skating, they are worth the extra money.

Within these two types, there are various kinds of roller skates. The difference often looks minor, but the changes make a big difference in how the skates perform and what you can use them for.

For example, one pair of skates may have narrow wheels. Another pair may have wide wheels. The wide wheels will give a smoother

Wide wheels like these give a smoother ride than narrow-wheeled skates.

ride. These wheels go over obstacles easier. And they are easier for beginners to stand up on, since they are spread over more area.

The wide wheels on skates work like the wide treads on a hot rod car. They put "more rubber on the ground," as the drag fans say. Only in the case of roller skates, it is more plastic on the ground. The most popular wheels today are made of polyurethane, a durable plastic. The extra surface and grip of these wheels give better traction. We can move faster with less effort.

Before you say, "That's for me!" let us point out that wide wheels also have disadvantages. You do not have the control with them in figure skating and spins that you have with narrow wheels. And, of course, they cost more.

Skates may differ in other ways, too. One pair may have a single cushion. Another pair may have double cushions. Wheels may be hard (for rink skates) or softer (for outdoor skating). There may also be a difference in the kind of bearing used. And so on. What kind of skates you use depends a lot on the kind of skating you do.

The Parts of a Skate

Except for the clamps and strap, the basic parts of the boot skate and the standard skate are the same. They are:

The truck assembly is shown in this bottom view of a skate. The axle hanger holds the wheel axle. The pivot arm is molded to the axle hanger and fits into a rubber grommet just below the toestop. Below the axle hanger is the cushion. The slot in the end of the cushion king pin permits adjusting the rubber spacers in the cushion for easy or firmer "action."

1. *THE PLATE*. This is the metal top piece. It serves as the place for the shoe sole to ride and for attachment of the wheels and supporting parts.

2. *THE TRUCK ASSEMBLY*. The truck is the assembly of parts that holds the wheels to the plate and affords the skater control over the skates. The parts that make up the complete truck assembly are:

a. *The Hanger*. This is a metal casing that holds the wheel axle to the skate plate. It is attached to the plate by the pivot arm and the king pin in the cushion assembly.

b. *The Pivot*. This is an arm molded to the hanger. It joins the skate plate at the pivot point where a rubber grommet provides a small amount of play. This pivot or movement helps the plate lean which provides the "rocking" that enables a skate to curve.

c. *The Cushion*. The cushion assembly is either one or two rubber pads. They are placed on each side of a spacer molded to the opposite side of the hanger from the pivot arm. A king pin holds the rubber pads in place and screws into the skate plate to hold the hanger in place. When the skater's foot leans and presses on the side of the skate, these rubber cushions compress, causing the skate to roll on a curve. This is called a skate's "action."

3. *THE WHEELS*. These may be polyurethane plastic, metal or wooden, depending on what they are used for.

These are the major parts. In addition there are assorted straps, clamps, washers and the like.

How to Choose Your Skates

Since skates are used for different purposes, a beginner sometimes has a problem deciding which kind of skate to buy. A good way to do it is to talk it over with the pro at the nearest skating rink. Tell him or her what you want to do, and where you intend to practice. These pros are professional teachers and all have had wide backgrounds in skating. Many are former champions in different branches of skating. They can not only tell you what kind of skates you need, but can also tell you the best brands.

If you don't want to go this route, then talk to an experienced skater who is doing the type of thing you want to do. Ask his or her advice. You'll find most of them are delighted to help out a beginner. However, nobody is perfect and even champions disagree on what is the

best model, brand or type. So it is always well to get several opinions.

Rental Skates

If you are just out for a little rolling fun and do not intend to take up skating seriously, then you may not need to buy skates at all. Roller rinks have boot skates you can rent. They will be the right type for the rink.

Amusement places, boardwalks and some parks also have rental skates. However, if you are going into any kind of competition or exhibition skating, you should have your own skates. You will get used to them. You will

Skates can be rented at skate shops which abound in recreational areas. They can also be rented at skating rinks. Rental skates are fine for weekend or occasional skating, but if you are serious about the sport, you should buy your own. It is also cheaper to own your own.

know what they can do. And you will do a better job of skating with them.

Indoor and Outdoor Skates

The difference between indoor and outdoor skates is in the type of wheels used. Originally skate wheels were made of metal or wood. Maple was a favorite for wooden wheels where something softer than metal was needed. Then in the 1960s polyurethane, a tough plastic, was developed. It can be made either hard or soft, and has quickly become a favorite for skate wheels.

The old metal wheels were bumpy. They had no give and made for an uneven ride that could be dangerous on anything except a smooth track. The newer polyurethane wheels come in a soft model for outdoor skating, and a harder wheel for indoor skating. The softer outdoor polyurethane wheels are more like rubber. They roll easily over pebbles, cracks and bumps that would flip-flop a skater on the old metal wheels. The "give" of the soft plastic causes the wheels to grip better on uneven surfaces. Also, they are not as noisy as hard wheels and the softer plastic absorbs a lot of the shock, making for a more pleasant ride.

On the debit side, they do not roll as fast as hard wheels. Being softer, they wear out more quickly. Since they are more expensive in the first place, this early wear adds to the cost.

The polyurethane wheel has become the skater's favorite. It is softer than metal and grips the pavement better. It comes in a softer model for outdoor skating and a harder model for indoor rinks.

These disadvantages are balanced by the definitely increased safety and smoother ride of the softer wheels.

Hard Polyurethane Wheels

There is a harder polyurethane wheel for indoor rinks. It does not ride as well on the outside as the softer wheel, for it rolls *over* puddles and obstructions, and does not grip the pavement as well as the softer wheel. This sometimes makes for a very slippery ride.

Outdoor polyurethane soft wheels are the same type of wheel used on skateboards. You can swap them around from skate to board.

The Indoor Skate

Indoor skating, which once favored wooden wheels, now prefers the hard polyurethane. They give a good grip on the smooth rink floors and last longer than the softer wheel preferred for outdoor skating. They are also easier to control and you can cut figures with them that would be more difficult on a softer wheel.

If you do both outdoor and indoor skating and just can't manage skates for each, then your best bet is to compromise on the harder wheel. You will just have to be more careful on the sidewalks, for these hard wheels are slippery on uneven surfaces. You'll also get a harder ride that is more tiring than rolling around on the softer wheels.

As far as width of the wheels goes, we noted earlier that you can go faster with less effort on the wider wheels. They do not maneuver as well as narrower wheels and you had best stick to the skinnier ones for figure skating and special exhibitions. And you'll save a little money in doing so.

You can buy spare wheels and it is only a matter of loosening the retaining nuts to slip

Here a wheel has been removed to show the axle shaft which goes through the hanger portion of the truck assembly. Wheels are easily removed and exchanged by loosening the retaining lock nut.

one kind off and slip another in its place. So there is really no excuse for not rolling along on the wheels that suit you best for the particular kind of skating you are doing.

Incidentally, polyurethane also holds better on wet pavement than the old steel wheels, but wet pavement can be dangerous with any kind of skate.

Getting Your Bearings

Your wheels are no better than their bearings. Bearings are the little steel balls in the wheel hubs that roll around the axle. Their job is to reduce friction. This eliminates a lot of

This shows the flat inside of a polyurethane wheel. The bearing in the center is the sealed type. It does not have to be cleaned as often as the loose bearings.

wear on both hub and axle, and lets you move faster with less effort.

Each wheel has two sets of ball bearings. The least expensive wheels use open bearings. They are good enough. However, being more exposed to dirt and grit, they have to be cleaned frequently to prevent excessive wear. Dirty bearings also cause undue friction which makes the wheels harder to turn.

The races—tracks in which the steel bearing balls move—are sealed with metal shields in closed-type bearings. This keeps in the lubricant and prevents grime from working its way in between the steel balls. These types of bearings are advertised as never needing cleaning or lubrication. This is not always true, but they certainly minimize maintenance care.

Sealed bearings are much more expensive

than the open variety. However, their longer life, less need for maintenance, and higher speed at the top end of the bracket make them worth the extra money they cost you.

Trucking Along

The truck, as we defined earlier, is the connecting link between the wheels and the skate plate. Originally it was only a hanger for fastening the wheels to the sole plate. It still does that, of course, but it also acts as shock ab-

This is a double-action truck cushion. It has two rubber pads in the assembly. Double cushions make leaning easier.

sorber to give us a less bumpy ride than earlier skates did.

More important than the easy-ride feature, the rubber cushions let the plates lean more easily when the skater applies foot pressure on the edges. This is the whole secret of the splendid maneuverability of modern skates.

Truck cushions come in two types. One is "single action." The other is "double action." What that means is this: The rubber for the cushion is mounted in a rod or axle that connects to an arm on the truck at the axle point, and to the skate plate at the other end. Single action cushions have one rubber disk and double action cushions have two rubber sections.

There are two cushions for each set of wheels—one in the front and one in the back. When your body leans, pressure is applied through the edge of the plate. This compresses the rubber disks—front and back—on that side. This causes the skate to curve in that direction.

This is the principle of Plimpton's rocking skate. Incidentally, Plimpton did not originate the term "rocking skate." It is supposed to have been coined by Charles Dickens, the man who wrote *Oliver Twist*. Dickens was a magazine editor and wrote an enthusiastic article about the new skates.

The cushions can be adjusted for tighter or looser action. Details on how this is done are in the chapter on skate care.

CHAPTER 3

SAFE SKATING

Skaters fall. Let there be no mistake about that. You can take some pretty hard lumps and pick up quite a bit of skinned hide. Yet, for all of this you don't hear of a lot of people getting seriously hurt, even though they take their spills on concrete or hard wood. Most of the injuries that do occur are the result of carelessness or disregard of basic safety rules.

Smaller children actually have it better than people who have reached their full size. This is because a smaller person has less distance to fall.

There are many ways to fall on a pair of skates. The most common, however, are a forward sprawl that spreads you right over the landscape, a backward sprawl that is likely to bounce your skull on the pavement, a sit-down where your feet slip out from under you and you plop your fanny hard against the track and a forward drop to your knees.

Taking Care of Yourself in a Fall

Falls should not shake you up badly. You can minimize the bumps by wearing proper protective clothing, and by learning how to fall. Protective clothing is something everyone can understand. But when you spring this "learning how to fall" on a lot of beginners, you get some hoots and attempts at humor.

"Forget that," I've had them tell me. "You don't need to teach *me* how to fall. That comes naturally to me!"

Falling *the wrong way* comes naturally to all of us. Falling the right way comes from hard practice in following a few basic rules.

Have you seen an actor get swatted in the face, stumble back and roll down a flight of stairs? Or maybe he got shot off a horse, hit the ground and tumbled down a canyon? Well, he didn't get clipped. The blow just grazed his face close enough for it to look like the real thing to the audience. The shot was a blank in the killing scene. *But*—in both cases the fall was real enough and sufficient to send any of us ordinary people to the intensive care ward.

Occasionally one of the stunt men who does this work does break his neck, but usually they walk away from the worst kind of fall without even a bruise.

The secret is that they know how to fall the right way. And there is no reason why skaters should not use a few of the stunt man's tricks

A good example of protective clothing is these knee protectors. They afford this bare-legged skater more protection than the long pants of her companions.

to ease the wear and tear on his own hide. There are really no secrets about them. They came right out of gymnastics and tumbling.

How to Fall

The secret of falling without injury is in using your body as a shock absorber. There is a simple experiment that shows how this is done. Here it is:

• Stand on a chair and jump down to the floor. Keep your legs stiff and land flat-footed.

• Note the shock that jars up through your entire body when your feet hit the floor.

• Now climb back on the chair and repeat the jump, but this time don't hold your legs so stiff. Let them flex at the knees, and land on the balls of your feet instead of flat-footed.

• You will notice much less shock this time. Both your feet and your legs acted as shock absorbers. There was "give" when the balls of your feet hit the ground and then let your heels down more slowly. The flexing of your knees also absorbed shock that went right up your spine when you landed flat-footed. You very effectively cushioned the shock.

This is a very simplified example of what gymnasts and stunt men mean when they speak of breaking a fall.

Controlling Force

Now let's apply this principle to a specific fall in skating. Suppose our skate hits a crack in the pavement. The skate stops. We keep going. It looks like we are going to splatter ourselves flat on the concrete. Our experimental jumping from the chair has shown us how shocking it can be to land hard and flat.

We can't do much about how hard we land, for that depends upon the force behind our fall. If we are really scooting when we take the tumble, there will be considerable force pushing us down. But while we can't do anything to lessen the original force, we can *spread it out* so that we are not subjected to the full jar at once.

The normal reaction when one feels himself falling is to stick out his arms to break the fall.

The idea is good. You want to get some kind of protection between your head and the pavement. Unfortunately, trying to stiff-arm your way out of the bump can lead to broken arms, or badly skinned palms at best. Hitting the concrete with outstretched palms may not be much different from rubbing them with a grindstone.

There are times, of course, when it is desirable to break your fall with your hands. When you do this, however, remember your chair jumping experiment. Don't keep your arms stiff. Flex the elbow. This will provide a spring action that will absorb some of the force from both your hands and arms, and from your body.

Distributing the Force

You can further lighten the bump by distributing the force over a longer period of time and a greater area of your body.

To show how this can be done, there is another experiment. If a person stands on any moving object and jumps to the ground flat-footed, he will probably fall flat on his own face.

The reason for this is a physical law relating to moving bodies. This law states that when something is moving it wants to keep moving. If it is stopped, it wants to stay stopped. It takes quite a bit of effort to overcome this stubborn attitude of nature.

When we jump off a rapidly moving platform of any kind, we are the moving body. When we hit the ground our body still wants to keep moving because of the force behind it. This force is expended in one big bang and we get quite a jar.

But, following the law of moving bodies, if we hit the ground *running,* we will wear off the extra force through continued movement. We get no banging up at all.

The Forward Shoulder Roll

Translating this to skating, we can imagine a situation where we are falling forward. This could be caused by hitting an obstruction in the pavement, by jamming the toestop down too hard and fast, or even by trying to show off. What we want to do is break the force of the fall as much as possible, and to *keep moving*.

We can do this with a gymnastic maneuver called the forward shoulder roll. It is sometimes called the football roll because it is a standard tactic on the gridiron where falling is part of the game.

Here is the step-by-step procedure:

1. When you feel yourself falling, get the right shoulder down. Turn your face to one side. This is so that if your head does hit the ground you will take the blow on the side of your face, instead of ramming your nose into the concrete.

2. Extend your right arm. It is vital that the *elbow be bent*. It will be disastrous to hit with the arm stiff and straight. You'll take the full jar on it. This arm is not supposed to absorb all the force of the fall. It is just a spring, a mild shock absorber to reduce some of the shock so that your shoulder, which hits next, will not have to take the full force itself.

3. *Give* when the hand strikes the ground, flexing at the elbow to provide spring action, while letting the right dropping shoulder come down to the ground to take most of the blow.

4. Let your body come on over the shoulder. You are actually doing a somersault on your right shoulder. I am sure that there has never been a child who has not turned somersaults in his or her time. It is the same thing, except you roll over on your shoulder instead of on the back of your neck. This is the right shoulder in this example, but may be the left shoulder if you are falling to the left side.

5. As you come over on your back, swing your arms around so you can press your hands hard against the ground. At the same time flex your knees and straighten your back. The combination of your forward roll and the extra pressure of your pushing hands should take you easily back on your feet again.

Easing the Bumps

What we have done is spread the shock and force of a hard fall over a longer time and more distance. The shock on any one part of the body may be reduced as much as ten to one. This can easily mean the difference between getting hurt and getting up laughing.

The forward shoulder roll is just one of many gymnastic tricks that a skater can learn to make things safer for himself. It would be a distinct advantage if all skaters would take a short course in tumbling. The ability to protect yourself in a fall is an obvious use for it. Gymnastics can be to your advantage in developing freestyle skating routines as well.

The rolls, falls, jumps, handstands and such that you learn in gymnastics can often be adapted to skating tricks. This is what the skating clowns you sometimes see in circuses have done. I recall once seeing a vaudeville act that was built entirely around gymnastics and tumbling on skates. The two performers took falls and did stunts that were absolutely stunning. They would have killed an ordinary skater, I'm sure. But they were just routine to these two because *they knew how to fall*. And this came right out of tumbling.

A Backward Fall

If your feet go out from under you—a not uncommon occurrence for a beginner—your best bet is to try and just sit down. This will throw all the shock on your rear end. In many people this is well padded and able to take the shock. Those with skinny rumps might be well advised to put a seat pad in their pants.

The main thing in a backward fall is to avoid hitting your head on the concrete or wooden rink floor. If you can't just sit down, then roll as you did in the forward roll, except backward. Hit on your rump if you can, tucking your head forward with your chin on your chest. Then roll over on your back and the back of your head and bring your tucked knees over for a full backward somersault.

"But when you fall you haven't got time for all that thinking," I've heard a number of beginners protest.

And they are absolutely right. You do not have time to think during a hard fall, because it is on you and over before you can ponder the matter. Therefore, you have to practice your tumbling routines until you can do them automatically without thinking. It is all a matter of practice.

The twists and turns of gymnastics and tumbling can put a kink in one's back very easily if you don't know what you are doing. Tumbling instructors always insist that no student beginner practice without a spotter to guide him through the routines. We also do not recommend that you practice gymnastics without an instructor to point you in the right way.

Proper Equipment

Knowing how to protect yourself when you fall is important. But it is also important to avoid falling if you can. And, while we cannot avoid all accidents, most falls can be avoided.

One way is to make sure your skates are in the best possible condition. Details on that are in the following chapter on skate care. So now we will just mention a few generalities.

1. Check your wheel bearings for free rotation. A broken bearing or rust inside the bearing may cause a wheel to jam. This can cause an unexpected twist to throw you to one side. You can take a serious fall this way, and even knock down a skating partner to cause a double accident.

2. Check your wheels for cracks. Polyurethane is pretty durable, but everything gets old. There are still some metal and wooden wheels around.

3. Check plastic and wooden wheels for embedded grime. Soft polyurethane wheels have excellent gripping qualities, but wheels used outdoors can become embedded with dirt and ground rock. This can, on certain surfaces, cause the wheels to slip.

4. There is also danger in riding on wet surfaces. It is easy to skid. This is especially true when skating on streets after rains. Water penetrating into pores of the pavement causes the

oil drippings to float to the surface. This can make the pavement very slippery.

5. A very good safety tip is to ride your skate track slowly the first time around on an outdoor run. Watch for cracks in the pavement, obstructions, slick areas and anything else that might cause trouble. This is no guarantee that someone won't come along and drop a banana peel on the skate path in front of you. But it helps eliminate a lot of surprises.

6. Don't try to do more than you know how. Leave the fancy skating to the experts until you have had a lot of practice.

7. Do not try to go too fast. Some of the most beautiful and fancy skating is done at a comparatively slow speed. Unless you are going in for speed skating in races, take it more easily and work for smoothness in your movements and grace in your actions. Skaters have been clocked at better than 25 miles per hour—and that is fast enough to get you a speeding ticket in some places. Recklessness on skates in a crowded area not only calls for a police citation, it deserves one.

8. A very important point is warm up before doing any strenuous skating. This is not so important if you only intend to take a rolling stroll down the boardwalk to look at the ocean. But if you are going to run some slaloms, have a race with some friends, kick out with some frantic disco dancing, or run a few of the more

difficult figure or freestyle routines, you will do your body a favor and probably do a better skating job if you limber up a little first. A few of the simpler stretching calisthenics are good enough. You don't have to remove your skates. Try a few deep knee bends, some trunk twists, and see if you can touch the ground with the tips of your fingers without bending your knees (and without having the skates flip out from under you, of course).

9. Skate only where you are supposed to. Many cities and towns have laws restricting where you can skate. Streets are out, except in some resort areas where streets are closed to all except pedestrians, bikes and skates. Bike paths are barred to skaters in some places and open to them in others. You have to watch for signs on this. In the Los Angeles area, skaters are barred from bike paths along the coast in Venice, but two miles down the beach they are permitted in another beach area. Roller rinks are the safest place to skate.

Proper Clothing for Skating

You will see skaters rolling along wearing everything from bikinis and bathing suits to fancy costumes and padded uniforms. What you need to wear depends a lot on the kind of skating you do. You don't need to be bundled up like a hockey goalie unless you are going to play roller hockey. On the other hand, a bikini is not recommended for a beginner.

Elbow protectors should be among the articles of protective clothing you wear.

Ideally, a beginner would wear—both male and female—a good stout pair of slacks. Jeans are fine, but not the tight, form-fitting kind. They don't always give you enough freedom of movement. Double-knit garments that stretch are much better.

Then to the slacks add a jacket that will also serve as a buffer if you fall. Knee pads that slip over your pants will be a big help. You might also use elbow pads, and gloves are invaluable. They permit you to break falls with your hands without danger of scraping off some hide. It is also a good idea to wear a helmet.

You see a lot of knee and elbow protectors worn, but few want to bother with helmets and gloves. This is unfortunate, for both really help a beginner.

If you don't like to wear protective clothing, it can be discarded as you gain experience and confidence. In the beginning, we recommend it strongly. You don't hear of a lot of injuries in skating, but even so, a beginner does take his lumps. Protective clothing—along with knowledge of how to fall properly—will minimize injuries. Why accumulate bruises you don't have to?

Shoes and Safety

The old clamp-on skates sometimes posed a danger. These clamped the skate plate to your regular shoe. Sometimes the clamp worked loose, broke, or your shoe sole worked out of it. Then you suddenly lost a skate.

The present style of boot skate, which has the boot attached to the skate plate and wheels, eliminates this danger. There are still some of the clamp type around, but shun them if you can. Also, the boot gives more support to your ankles. You are less likely to turn an ankle with them.

CHAPTER 4

LEARNING TO SKATE

When you see someone swinging down the street on skates, it looks easy. Then you put on your first pair and try to stand up. Suddenly it does not seem easy anymore. It is like standing on a greased ball. Your feet want to go every way but right.

All this is normal. It happens to most of us when we put on our first skate. You have only made one mistake. That is changing your mind about skating being easy, for it *is* easy. Never mind any uneasy feeling that the world isn't solid anymore. All you lack is confidence, and that will come as soon as you find that you really can stand up on a pair of skates.

The First Step

If you strap on a pair of skates and try to shove off with no other preparation, you are likely to be picking yourself up before you have gone two feet. The first thing a beginner must do is learn how to stand.

Keeping your balance is your first problem when you stand on skates for the first time. Use your hands to help keep your balance.

Standing up on skates is all a matter of balance. You can take a stick and make it stand up in the palm of your hand in spite of gravity—if you can balance it properly. It is the same with your upright body on a pair of skates.

But even before you take that first step on wheels, you have to put the skates on. The skates should be the same size as the shoes you wear, but try them on to see if they fit. Every manufacturer can't measure as well as the other and marked sizes don't always come out the same with different companies.

Skates should have a snug fit, but should not be so tight as to be uncomfortable. Lace them all the way to the top to provide ankle support.

Most skates have eyelets for lacing about halfway up the boot. The rest of the lacing is done with hooks to speed things up so you can get moving faster.

You are going to have enough trouble keeping your balance at first, so lace your boots tightly. You don't want your foot slipping around inside when you try to stroke, turn and stop. However, you do not want the lacing so tight that it is going to be uncomfortable or cut off circulation in your feet. A good snug comfortable fit is enough.

This done, you are now ready for the first step in learning to skate. This actually isn't a step at all. It is just learning to stand—and balance yourself.

Wheeled Stand

Different instructors have their own methods of starting out a beginner. One I know has his students hold to the guard rail in the skating rink. Then with one hand still on the rail for support, he has them walk on their skates. They are instructed to take small steps, placing the four wheels solidly on the rink floor. They are told to keep their backs absolutely straight and their feet close together. This is to maintain a straight down center of gravity and aid them in keeping their balance.

This entire routine is aimed at teaching the beginner that he can stand up on skates and

Your first problem is learning to stand on skates. Put your feet together with your weight on the balls of your feet. Learn to stand before you try to move. Use your hands to help balance yourself.

giving him experience in maintaining balance.

After the student can do this with confidence, the instructor has him do the same thing without holding to the rail.

Another instructor refuses to let his students hang on to the rail at all. It's "cold turkey" all the way with him. Fortunately, he is not a cruel man. He stands beside the student ready to put out a helpful, balancing hand if one is needed. He does not have any more students fall than the instructor who permits them to hang onto the rail.

Still another way, and probably the best, is to use the rail and just pull yourself along, instead of walking as in the first method. Don't go far. Two or three feet are enough. All you need to show here is that you can stand up on skates and can move forward. Keep your weight on the forward part of the skate. Don't do this by leaning your body. Your body must remain straight to maintain your balance. Flex your knees slightly to put the weight where it should be.

Continue this pulling yourself forward a few feet at a time until your body gets accustomed to *balancing in motion*.

Next you repeat this, but shift weight from one foot to the other while pulling yourself along.

When you can do this, try removing your hand from the rail. Just pull the rail enough to get yourself moving. Then take your hand off and coast. You can grab the rail if you start losing balance. When you can roll without tottering, practice shifting weight from one foot to the other while rolling.

When you can balance yourself on rolling skates, and shift back and forth between them without falling, all you have to do is learn to stroke and you are skating!

Just how long you have to be a railbird depends upon your natural sense of balance.

Some get the hang of balancing rapidly. There are others who take three hours or more of continued practice.

Don't cut this practice short. It is the rock upon which you will build everything else you may do on skates.

The Difference Between Walking and Skating

Everyone has seen skaters. Perhaps you have watched a lot of them or you would not have decided to become a skater yourself. But the trouble is you have probably *watched* them without really *seeing* what they are doing. In other words, too many nonskaters do not look for the little things that skaters do that make skating skating.

You can see this because too many beginners try to walk on skates or shove themselves along when they first put a pair of wheels on their feet.

The technique of skating and the technique of walking are quite different.

A person walking steps forward on one foot. The full weight of the body shifts to this foot. The other knee flexes, raising that foot while leg muscles swing it forward of the supporting foot. The moving foot touches the ground and the body weight shifts to it as the former supporting foot now begins its swinging cycle. The feet are shifted one after another directly in front of the walker as he proceeds on a forward straight line.

In skating, you push yourself along. In the above photo, the skater is rolling forward on his left foot (right as viewed by the reader). His other foot—which is the "pushing foot"—is shoved backward and slightly to the side. This provides the push to make the skater move ahead. The slight sidewise turn of the skate is necessary to provide traction. Otherwise, the foot would just roll backward and give no "push."

But now stand and observe a skater. He does *not* place one skate directly in front of the other as a walker does his feet. Nor does he roll smoothly straight ahead. He moves forward on his skates, to be sure. But he *rolls ahead on one skate* while pushing *backward and slightly to the side* of the other foot.

What he is doing is shoving himself along with one *pushing* foot while rolling forward on the other skate. If you watch closely, you will see that a skater does not move directly ahead.

He proceeds in a series of slightly curved strokes.

Skating Step-by-Step

Here is a step-by-step outline of the starting procedure. For this demonstration, we will start moving on the *left* foot in a forward line. You may start on the right if it is more natural.

In this demonstration, our left foot is the *employed* or *carrying* foot. Regardless of which term you use, it means the same thing. The carrying foot is the foot or skate that is carrying the weight of your body in this particular step.

Your other—right—foot in this case is your *pushing foot*. It is the foot that will push you off to get you rolling on your way. When this foot comes off the ground, it becomes the *free* foot.

1. Now stand with your feet together. If your toes are spread to make a V, it will make the next step a bit easier. If you do angle your feet, be sure the toe of the carrying foot is pointed in the direction you wish to roll.

2. Your body weight is on your left foot. Your left knee is slightly bent. Shift weight to your right (pushing foot) and push backward and slightly to the side, putting pressure on the *inside* front side of the skate. Since the pressure is on the side of the skate, there is resistance that pushes the skater forward.

3. The V position is necessary for the start

To start from a stop in skating, stand with your toes in a V and then push off with your "pushing foot." In the above photo, the right foot is the carrying foot, and the left is the pushing foot.

because if the two feet were parallel, the backward push would cause the pushing skate to roll back instead of offering the resistance needed to cause the carrying (right) skate to roll forward. Remember that the backward push is slightly sidewise and the foot pressure is on the inside of the foot.

4. When the pushing foot is straight back—as far as it can push—and you are rolling forward, lift the pushing leg to a forty-degree angle and rotate it around.

5. The leg in the air is called the *free leg* now. Bring it around so that it touches the ground before the forward speed from the first stroke falls off.

6. Shift weight to the right skate, turning it into the rolling foot. Press backward and

Here are two skaters rolling along. The woman's left foot (right as viewed by the reader) is the carrying foot. Her pushing foot is swinging around to become the new carrying foot. The man's carrying foot is his right (left to the viewer).

slightly to the side with the left leg, which is now the pushing leg. Keep the carrying knee slightly flexed to permit the pushing leg to do the most possible work.

7. This is a full right-left cycle. Keep repeating as you stroke your way down the street.

Balance in Motion

If you push hard, you will roll faster. However, in the beginning you are not concerned with how fast and how far you can go with a single push. The important thing is to learn to push and rotate and shift weight smoothly without losing balance.

Therefore, do not try to go too fast in the beginning. It is easy to lose balance if you try to jerk your free foot around too rapidly. Watch the position of your arms. They are an important factor in helping you maintain balance. Balance is simply distributing your weight to keep your center of balance along a perpendicular (straight up and down) axis. The shifts of your body and arms redistribute weight to help you maintain balance. Your balance point is the balls of your feet. Never try to balance on your heels. Balance on the ball of your *carrying* foot. Proper balance comes with practice. After a while, you will find it automatic. You'll balance without even thinking about it.

Curves and Turns

The secret of turning on skates is the *edge*. The term "edge" is used both for the edge of the skate and for the curve that results from skating on the edge of the skate.

Let us review for a moment what we said earlier about the trucks and cushions. The cushions are rubber pads attached to the truck assembly that holds and controls the wheels. The cushion assembly may have one rubber pad. This is a single action cushion. If there are two rubber pads, then it is a double action cushion.

Leaning to one side or the other causes these rubber pads to compress. How much the pads compress depends upon how much you lean (and how heavy you are, of course), and how tightly the cushion assembly is adjusted.

This compression, caused by the body weight on the side or edge of the skate, causes the skate to take a curved path. The more you lean and press, the more the skate will curve.

If we want to curve to the right, we lean on the outside of our right foot. If we want to curve left while riding on the same right foot, then we lean inside. That is, toward the instep of the right foot. This causes the skate to take a left edge.

This is all done on the right foot, but you can make similar inside and outside curves on the left foot as well.

The "action" of the truck can be adjusted by tightening (compressing) the rubber pads in the cushion assembly. This is done by screwing in the slotted king-pin bolt and by tightening the adjusting nut at the other end of the assembly. You can make tighter turns with a loose adjustment, but lack the control of a tight adjustment.

A curve made on the outside edge of your foot is an *outside* curve. A curve made on the instep side of your foot is called an *inside* curve.

The inside curve is more difficult because it requires putting your leaning weight on the weaker side of your foot. It is weaker because of the instep. On an outside curve you can put pressure on the skate edge from your little toe to your heel. But on an inside curve the pressure comes only from the ball and heel of your foot. The raised instep prevents the rest of the foot from touching.

The young skater on the left has just completed an inside curve on his right foot. The young woman is preparing for an outside curve on her left foot. Upsidedown plastic cups make their slalom course.

The Lean

We said earlier that the adjustment of the cushion, along with the amount of lean, controls the amount of curve the skate will make. You will have to make the cushion adjustments by trial and error to find out what is best for you. In the chapter on skate care we discuss the adjustments more fully. Double action cushions give more lean, but a one-cushion action gives better control for figure skating.

Leaning must be done just right. Keep your legs, trunk, shoulders and head in as straight a line as you can.

A lot of beginners have trouble leaning properly. They want to bend at the hips or bend forward or backward. The idea, however, is to keep the body as straight as possible and pivot on your foot.

The best way to practice this is on the floor without skates. Instead of consciously trying to lean your body, transfer weight by pressing hard on your carrying foot while easing up pressure on your opposite foot. This automatically makes you lean, if you are doing it right.

You don't need an extraordinary amount of lean. If your cushions are properly adjusted, a small amount of lean may produce enough curve for what you need.

Remember, you always lean in the direction you want to curve. And the lean is always to the side, never forward or backward. The more you lean and the looser your cushion adjustments, the smaller the circle you will trace.

The Mohawk Turn

An edge produces a curve. You can use it to produce a circle or a spin. You can also use the curve to make a wide, gentle turn. But if you need to get turned around in a hurry, you will have to try something else.

A skater uses a rail for balance while practicing the movements of a Mohawk Turn. Note that the body shifts along with the feet.

A simple, popular way to turn around is the Mohawk Turn. While skating forward, go into a gentle curve. Extend your free foot with the toe pointed *to the rear*. As you bring your free foot down to the skating surface, lift your carrying foot to transfer weight to the other foot, which now becomes the carrying or employed foot.

Rotate the former carrying foot, now the free leg, so that both feet are going the same way again. Stroke off and away you go.

Here is the Mohawk Turn in step-by-step outline:

1. Roll into a mild curve on the right inner edge foot. Turn the left free leg so the toe is pointing as much as possible in the direction you want to go.

2. Drop your left skate to the floor, letting your inner toe wheel touch down first.

3. As your weight comes on your left skate, lift your right skate and revolve it around beside your left one.

4. Lower your right skate to the floor and stroke off.

Stop!

The easiest way to halt is to use the toestop. This is the rubber plug on the front of your skates. Figure skates do not use toestops, but freestyle skates do.

If you raise your heel, tilting the skate for-

The skate is tilted forward to let the rubber toestop rub the ground. This skater is using his free skate for the brake.

Putting your free foot in a T behind your carrying foot will cause the back skate to drag and slow you to a stop. This is effective, but hard on your skate wheels.

71

ward, the rubber stop rubs against the ground to act as a brake. It has to be eased against the pavement to avoid pitching you off your skates.

The best way to use a toestop is to keep rolling on the carrying foot and gently use the free foot to do the braking. Be careful not to drag yourself to one side. You may have to bend back slightly to minimize the pitch of stopping.

If you do not have toestops, put your free skate behind your carrying skate to form a T. This puts the back skate crosswise so it can drag you to a stop.

CHAPTER 5

SIMPLE FIGURE SKATING

Figures take roller skating right back to its beginning—ice skating. You can do any figure on roller skates that an ice skater can do on his colder rink. You may not be able to do the figures as easily on roller skates as he can on ice skates, but you can do them with grace and beauty. At the same time you will be participating in a highly competitive sport that can lead to national and international championships.

There is a strong movement to get roller skating added to the list of Olympic Games events. It is already accepted by the Pan-American Games.

Figure skating breaks down into two distinct sections, both of which you must do in figure competitions. One is the Compulsory School Figures. These are basic figure-skating routines that everyone must do. There is some leeway in the way you do them, but what you do is locked in. This shows the judges that you have mastered the fundamentals of classic figure skating.

The second type you will be called upon to do in competitions is freestyle skating. This is still figure skating, but you make up your own routine within certain guidelines. You don't get too fancy dreaming up a routine or you'll end up with disco dancing or something even more far out.

Going in Circles

Figure skating is not as difficult as it appears to a beginner watching an expert make like a ballet dancer on wheels. As soon as you have achieved good balance and can skate a full circle, you are equipped with the technical ability to start learning your school figures.

And this means going around in circles. Skating a circle means just that, a *circle*. No goose eggs or wavering lines are permitted. If you have trouble staying in line, get a skating buddy to support you until you learn just how much lean and forward speed is necessary to make an edge that will follow the trace (the drawn line).

Some rinks have the required pattern lines painted on their floors. At home you can draw a chalk line on the patio or driveway for practice there.

Figure skating is akin to ballet dancing.

In order to follow the line exactly, you must have the right amount of body lean to get the correct amount of leg pressure on the edge of your skates. This is what you learned in making turns, but here you must be more exact. You are a slave to the line of the figure.

It is very easy to apply too much pressure and edge more than you should. This will cut you inside the circle. Or you may not apply enough pressure and swing wide of the line.

Ease Up, Bear Down

This is not too much of a problem. Ease up if you are cutting too tight a circle. Bear down on the edge a little more if you are going wide. Don't try to correct everything at once. Just ease up or bear down a little at a time so that you do not overcorrect. Retune your cushions if that helps.

At first your major concern is staying on the line. It is permissible to use more than one stroke in learning, but once you get experience you should be able to kick off and make the entire circle without additional stroking.

Figure Skates

Before going into the mechanics of your first figure—which will be the classic Figure (or Circle) 8—we had best talk about skates for school figures.

Note the use of the toestop on the dancer's forward foot in this freestyle dance routine.

Different types of skates are needed for school figures and for freestyle skating. This difference is mainly in the type of wheels used and the tuning of the cushions. Tuning is called "setting the action."

The wheels on figure skates are harder and more narrow than those for freestyle. They also have a somewhat different balance, which is caused by the placement of the bearings.

Figure skates do not have toestops, but you do use them on freestyle skates. The toestop on freestyle skates is not so much for stopping as for a brace to aid you in making jumps of the type used in some freestyle routines.

The action is harder on figure skates than on freestyle. This means you must tighten down on the cushion adjustments. Just how much is a matter of personal feel. Your body weight plays a part in it. Also your style of edging must be taken into consideration. Many figure skaters say make the adjustment as tight as you can, but not so much that you cannot lean the skate to make the curve. A good way to work out this problem is to tighten the nut too much and then slack off after each practice run until you have the action just right for your style.

General Purpose Skates

While everyone agrees that you need different style skates for school-figure and freestyle skating, they also agree that this is not necessary for students. The extra margin the correct skate gives you is not essential until you get into competition. Then, as in all competitions, you need every bit of help on your side.

Until then you can make one pair of skates do for practice in both styles. You may have to adjust the action, but, as you will learn in Chapter 9, that is not much trouble.

School Figure Circles

Compulsory school figures will keep you going around and around. They are always done on circles. The pattern consists of either two or three circles of equal size. They are six meters (19.8 feet) in diameter. Younger skaters may use a five meter circle (16.5 feet), for they are not strong enough to get around the larger circle with the smoothness and grace that competition skating demands.

These circles are painted on the rink floor in black to make them easily seen. They are one-half inch wide. The circles, whether a pattern of two or a pattern of three, are arranged in a straight line with their lines just touching at one point.

You must skate around the entire pattern in a definite manner as prescribed by the rules.

Diagram Notations

In doing any school figure you must skate around the circles in a definite manner. The

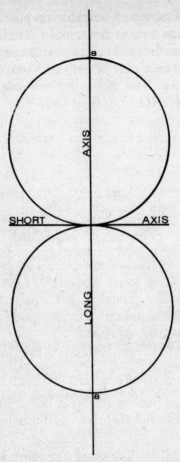

The Circle 8 (Figure 8) school figure is skated on two equal circles that touch at one point. An imaginary line drawn through the centers of the circles is the Long Axis. Another imaginary line drawn through the point where the circles touch is the Short Axis. These axis points are used to show you where to place your feet for the Circle-8 takeoff. The small "a" marks the apex points.

name of the figure will tell you how this will be done. The various text books on figure skating have diagrams that teach you the proper movements. These movements are listed in a written shorthand. You'll see such cryptic notations as: LOF, ROF, RIB and ROB.

After we get over our first bewilderment, these letters are easy to figure out. They tell you which foot to use, which side of the foot to edge, and which direction to skate around the circles.

Let's take LOF for a starter. The first letter is the foot you use to start on: Left. The second letter—O—tells us that the edge is on the outside of the left foot. The third letter—F—tells us that the direction is forward from the starting position. So, LOF means use the outside edge of your left foot to start and go forward.

If the notation was LOB, instead of LOF, it would mean: You start on your left foot, outside edge, and go *backward*. The B means backward. If the notation had been ROB, then it is the *right* foot, outside edge, and backward movement.

If the movement calls for an inside edge to make the curve, then the notation would read R or L, depending upon the foot to use, followed by an I for inside, and then an F or a B for forward or backward.

To sum up, in a simple diagram that can be easily referred to if you forget a letter:

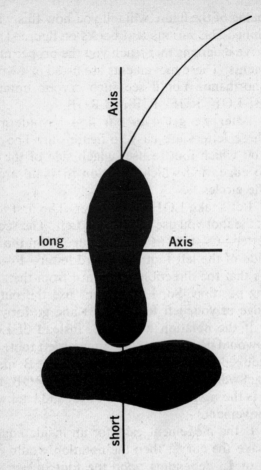

Axis

long   Axis

short

This would be the position for takeoff on a left inside forward (LIF) curve. Your weight would be on the inner (arch) side of your foot. The right foot, instep against left heel, is the pushing foot. Position carrying foot on short axis with long axis running through the left instep.

The *first* letter is the foot used.
The *second* letter is the edge used.
The *third* letter is direction skated.
L means left foot.
R means right foot.
O means outside edge.
I means inside edge.
B means backward.
F means forward.

Circle Symbols

The circles also have symbols to aid you and let you know where you are. These symbols are the same for both the two-circle designs and the three-circle designs.

Draw an imaginary line through the centers of the circles. This line is the "long axis."

Draw another imaginary line between the circles at the point where they touch. This line is the "short axis."

The point where the long axis crosses the top of the top circle is an "apex." The point where the long axis crosses the bottom line of the lower circle is also an "apex."

The only difference between the two-circle skating design and the three-circle design is that the three-circle one will have two "short-axis" points. These symbols permit you to read a diagram easily. They also permit an instructor to easily point out errors: "You cut in too much at the apex. Loosen up a little on the action.''

Also, each figure begins on the short axis at the point where the circles touch.

The Basic Circle 8 Pattern

All school figures are started from a stopped position. You have no chance to build up speed before you go into one. Therefore, you need to give yourself a good push on that initial take-off.

The position of your feet will vary according to the type of figure you are skating. In every case the toe of your carrying foot will be on the line and pointed in the direction you wish to skate. The pushing foot will be behind it, forming a T, so it can send you on your way.

The name of the figure tells you which foot you will put forward. The basic Circle 8 is a ROF-LOF figure. This means we will begin on the right foot and skate an outside edge. Then when we complete the first circle on this foot and edge, we will have to change legs to skate the second circle on the left leg and outside edge.

The start is called a takeoff. The change of feet is also known as a takeoff, but is generally called a "transition" in order not to be confusing.

Transitions, like your takeoff, must be done

The start in figure skating is called the "takeoff." This is an ROF movement; that is, right foot, outside edge, forward. The skater's hands should have been raised for this takeoff, with the index finger of the right hand on the line to be followed.

gracefully and smoothly. You will have to prepare for the change of foot and must begin getting ready for it so there will be no break in
your skating rhythm.

You start getting ready for the transition
about one-third of the way around the circle.
You do this by rotating (that is, bringing forward) your free leg. This brings it into position
to let you shift from your right leg to the left
when you complete the first circle.

At this point, you move your right leg
slightly off the line and bring your left leg down
on the line. Then your weight is shifted from
your right to your left leg.

Your right leg then becomes the free leg and
you roll around the second circle on this part
of the pattern on the outer edge of your left
foot. This fulfills the LOF requirement of the
basic Circle 8 figure.

What you have done is to skate the top or
right circle on the outer edge of your right foot,
and the second circle on the outer edge of your
left foot, making the change of feet without a
pause.

The Second Time Around

When you finish the second circle, you have
made a Figure 8, but you have not completed
the school figure. You must skate the pattern
twice before you are through. So when you get
back to the starting point at the short axis, you
shift feet again. Then riding again on the outer

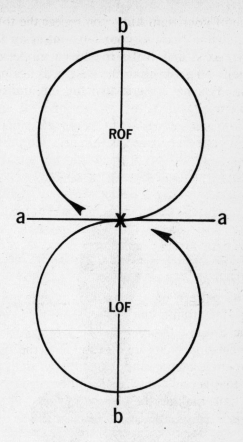

This is the basic pattern for the ROF-LOF compulsory school Circle 8 (Figure 8). Your takeoff is at the X point on the short axis (a—a). You skate to the right, rolling on the outer edge of your right foot. Circle the circle on this foot and return to X, the original takeoff point. At X you shift to your left foot, riding on the outer edge, to circle the lower circle. Since you must make two circuits of the pattern, you switch back to your right foot when you return to X and go around the two circles exactly as you did the first time.

edge of your right foot, you repeat the top circle, switch back to your left foot again at the short axis, and make the lower circle again. When you get back to the short axis again, that is it. You have made two full circuits of the pattern.

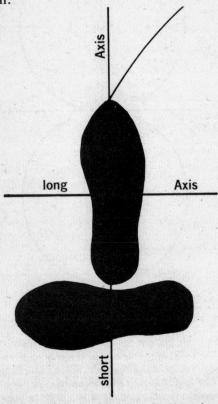

Here are the positions for your feet for the takeoff on the ROF-LOF Circle 8 figure. Your right foot is the carrying or employed foot. Your left foot is the pushing foot. The lean is outside.

Circle 8 Takeoff Step-by-Step

1. Place your right foot on the short axis. The long axis should run across the center of this foot.

2. Next place your left foot crosswise behind your right. The left instep should lightly touch the right heel to form a T with the other foot. This is the stationary position.

3. Raise your arms. The right arm is forward. The left arm is to the rear. The middle finger of your forward arm should be over the line you expect to skate.

4. Now take the poised position. To do this, raise your right skate from the floor. About four inches is right. Draw this foot back until the right instep is about at the heel of your pushing foot.

5. Flex your left knee. Push your weight forward on your right (carrying) foot as you push back with your left foot.

6. Your weight and lean are on the outer edge of your right foot to create the required ROF turn around the circle.

The Transition

The transition is the switch from a right carrying foot to a left carrying foot. This creates a small problem.

You do *not* put your left foot beside the right and lift up the right. The left skate must go

In making transitions from one foot to the other, do not swing your free leg out too far. Bring your free foot in until it is almost ankle-to-ankle with your carrying skate.

right on the line. In this particular spot you are permitted to move your right skate off the line. Ordinarily you are penalized if your foot strays off the line.

On the Circle 8 ROF-LOF that we have been talking about, your right skate curves *inside* the circle as you come down the outside edge of the right circle line. This must be done rapidly, but not so rapidly that it appears jerky or as if the skater made a hop. This inside curve should not extend more than two skate lengths. This is just enough time and space to permit you to put your left skate on the trace and set up a new edge to carry you along the left circle line.

ROF-LOF Circle 8 Step-by-Step

We have already made a general description of the ROF-LOF Circle (Figure) 8. However, as this is the first of the school figures and the easiest for beginners to do, here is a step-by-step guide for this basic figure:

1. Take a poised position, right skate on the trace line at the short axis. The left free leg is behind with the left skate forming a T with the right skate.

2. Flex your left knee and push your weight to your right foot. Lean your body to make the proper edge for the circle curve.

3. About one third of the way around the circle (some instructors say one quarter) begin moving your arms and free leg around in a smooth rotation. This is to put your leg and balance in position for the transition from skating on your right foot to skating on your left.

4. Do not swing your free leg and arm out too much. It is awkward and can cut your speed.

5. Lower your free leg smoothly until your free skate is almost ankle-to-ankle with the skating foot. You are now ready to make the switch from the right skating foot to the left skating foot.

6. As you come up to the short axis, cut slightly into the circle with your right skate to get off the line so you can lower your left skate to it and stroke a new edge.

7. You are now skating on the left foot with the right foot free, circling the lower or left circle of the pattern.

8. Then about a quarter or a third of the way around this second circle, you begin rotating your right leg and arm in preparation for the next transition, when you begin the second run around the twin circles.

Things to Watch For

All movements must be smooth, for grace is one of the most important points in figure skating. Avoid jerky movements. Make every movement flow. Learn to push off with sufficient speed to avoid wobbling at the end of a circle. Stay on the lines at all times, except for the brief transition periods. Hold your body straight, and do not lunge at the takeoff.

CHAPTER 6

MORE FIGURES AND FREESTYLE

The figure just described, right outside forward-left outside forward (ROF-LOF), begins to the right on the outside edge. By taking off from the same position—the point where the circles touch on the short axis—you can switch feet and go in the opposite direction.

This is the LOF-ROF—left outside forward-right outside forward. You will not be doing anything really new. You are just reversing the order in which you do them. That is, you skate the left circle first and then the right circle.

The starting position is different. Instead of the right foot place your left foot on the short axis and put your right foot behind it so that the heel of the left foot is even with the instep of the right foot. Draw up your knee on the left foot and slightly flex your right knee to take the poised position.

Then shove off on the left foot, leaning to

create the proper edge to keep you on the circle trace.

Beginners are permitted to stroke more than once to get speed to take them completely around the circle, but you should strive to get enough in that first takeoff to move you all the way around.

In the first half of this version of the Circle 8, you are rolling to the left on the outside edge of your skate going forward or in skater's symbols: LOF.

When you circle back to the short axis on this initial round, you switch feet. Having already started rotating your free leg, you bring it around and down on the trace as you move your left skate out of the way by a slight inward turn at the short axis. Bring your right foot down on the trace in its place and skate away ROF. When you return to the short axis, switch to the left foot and begin the second run over the twin circles. This is a completely different school figure, but you can see that as far as movements go you only have to get used to starting on a different foot. The rest is identical. All you need is practice—and never mind the kibitzers. They all had to learn themselves.

Variations

We will now try some variations of the basic Circle 8. We will still make two turns around the twin circles, but this time we will do them

This is the takeoff foot position for the LOF—left foot, outside edge forward circle movement.

on the *inside edge*. Some skaters find the inside edge more difficult because this is the arched side of the foot. When you lean to create the edge, all the pressure you put on the skate plate is transmitted through your heel and the ball of your foot. You are pressing against your raised arch.

These school figures are graceful exhibitions in their own right as you skate first this way and then that way. But they are also the foundation upon which you will build everything else you do in skating. This is true whether you are doing disco dancing, roller hockey, freestyle or just Sunday skating in the park. They all require curves, inside and outside edges, change of feet, starting and stopping. So it is very important that you learn and practice your school figures as much as possible, even if you do not intend to enter competitions.

Since each one is only a slight variation from the preceding one, all you have to do is just add gradually as you progress. This makes learning an easy task, as you go forward step-by-step. Each new step will be easy if you have thoroughly learned the ones that come before it. In a surprisingly short time you will be whizzing around circles with the best of them.

The Insiders

For our first insider let's skate the RIF-LIF Circle 8. This is school figure number 2.

This is a right inside forward pushoff. The

If you feel like tap dancing on skates, go ahead! From Disco to Ballet, dancing on skates is the new fad.

right foot is the carrying foot. The left foot is the pushing foot and then the free foot or leg.

In this figure we will push off to the *left* and *ride the left* or *lower circle,* circling back to the short axis where we will change feet and circle up around the right or top circle to return to the short axis where we will repeat the two circles again.

The difference between this and ROF-LOF school Circle 8 number 1 is that we use different feet for each circle. In the first figure we went around the top circle on the outside edge of our right foot. Then at the short axis we switched to our left foot. If we had not switched to the left, it would have been necessary to turn our lean and ride the lower circle on the inside edge. So we changed to the left foot to permit following the trace with the outside edge as the figure direction requires.

In figure number 2 we must ride both circle traces on the inside edge. So we merely reverse the feet and circles we start with. Otherwise, everything is the same.

We are just going around in circles as we did before. All you have to learn is to lean in the opposite direction and put a different foot out at the start.

The RIF-LIF Circle 8

1. Take the standard stationary position on the short axis between the right and left circles. The name of the figure (RIF-LIF) tells you which foot to put first. It is the right and we will edge on the inside of the foot in a forward motion.

2. Extend your arms front and back. The left arm is extended to the front. Draw your right foot back in the poised position, slightly raised from the floor.

3. Bend your carrying leg slightly so you can get leverage for the pushoff.

4. Bring your right skate down on the trace while shoving back with your left foot to get a good sendoff. Watch your lean and the posi-

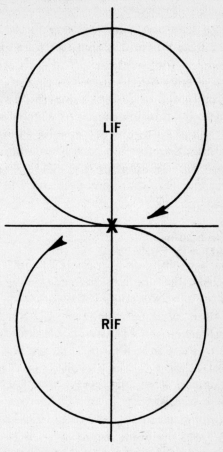

This is the RIF-LIF Circle 8, which is skated on the inside edge. If you compare it with the pattern for the ROF-LOF, you will see that it is the same except that you start in a different direction and skate on the inside instead of the outside of your right and then your left foot. All you have done is change the foot and direction.

tions of your arms and shoulders to create a proper inside edge.

5. Rotate your free leg around as in the other Circle 8 figures to prepare for a handoff to your left foot at the short axis to continue an inside edge for the upper or right circle.

If you intend to go into competition skating, you will need an instructor to watch for your little faults and to correct mistakes that seem unimportant, but which cost you points. But if you are only skating for fun, who cares? Sail around any way that suits you and which you find easy.

The Serpentine

The Serpentine is a dramatic skating figure, but is actually simple to do once you have mastered the Circle 8. Where the previous figures have used twin-circle patterns, the Serpentine uses three circles. They are the same size as those of the Circle 8 family and are laid out in a line so that they touch each other. The Serpentine is known as ROIF-LIOF school figure number 5.

From the symbols you can see what feet and edges you are going to have to use. ROIF means right foot, outside-inside edge, forward. From this you can see that you are going to have to combine in one figure the techniques of both the ROF-LOF and the RIF-LIF Circle 8s that you just learned. Here again, we are

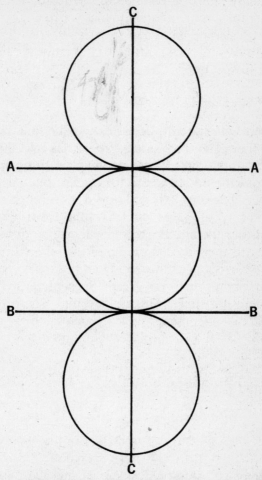

The Serpentine school figures are skated on a three-circle trace. A—A and B—B are the two short axes in this pattern. C—C is the long axis. The axes are your reference points. They are imaginary lines and do not appear on the rink floor.

actually doing nothing new. We are merely combining and extending what we have previously learned in order to present something that will look new, different and more difficult to the spectators.

The Serpentine Basic Form

We will skate the Serpentine in the following manner: The three-circle pattern has two short axes—the points where an imaginary line cuts across the points where the circles touch each other. The long axis still runs right through the center of all three circles. Some instructors consider the circles as being sideways. Others refer to them as one on top of the other. If we consider them as stacked from bottom to top, you begin the ROIF-LIOF Serpentine at the lower short axis. This is the point where the bottom and middle circles touch each other. This was the same place you started the first Circle 8.

Step-by-step, the ROIF-LIOF Serpentine is skated in this way:

1. Take your position on the short axis where circles 1 and 2 touch.

2. The position of your feet is the same as for the ROF-LOF Circle 8 takeoff. That is, you place your right skate on the short axis with your body facing left so you will get an outside edge as you roll clockwise up the middle (number 2) circle.

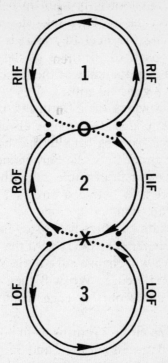

This is the track pattern for the ROIF-LIOF Serpentine. The three inner circles are the ones you skate. The dotted lines are where you cross your old trace as you come back around. The partial circles outside the circles you skate show the portions of those circles that you skate with which foot, edge and direction. Start at X, skating right on *circle 2* ROF to 0. At 0 change from outer edge (ROF) to inner edge (RIF) and skate the entire *circle 3* on RIF. When you return to 0, change to your *left inner* edge (LIF) and skate the second half of *circle 2*. At X you will have completed both circles 2 and 3. At X change to your left outer edge (LOF), circling *circle 1* and coming back to X. At X, shift back to ROF to repeat the Serpentine.

3. Your left foot is brought in behind your right to form the T. Then take the poised position, raising the heel of the right foot and drawing it back to the heel of the left foot, slightly bending the knee of the left or pushing foot to get a good takeoff.

4. Here is where the difference comes in. In the Circle 8, you skated completely around circle number 2, coming back to the short axis to change for circle 1. In the Serpentine, we will only skate one-half of circle 2 and then switch at the short axis between circles 2 and 3 to skate the top (number 3) circle.

5. We skate the first half of circle 2 clockwise on an outer edge (ROF). At the short axis (point O) we will change edge to the right inner forward (RIF) edge. We will then skate the entire top circle on this edge, going counterclockwise.

6. Circling circle 3 returns us to point O, the short axis between circles 2 and 3.

7. Here we change to the left foot, skating LIF—left inner forward—to complete the other half of circle 2. We roll this trace in a clockwise direction. This brings us back to point X on the diagram.

8. We are now at the short axis between circles 1 and 2 (point X). Here we shift edge again to LOF—left outer forward, rolling counterclockwise on the lower circle. We completely trace circle 1 on the left outer edge and return

to X to complete the three-circle pattern. Then we repeat the entire pattern.

What We Did

A description of a movement like this sounds confusing, but if you trace the movements on the accompanying diagram, it should become clear to you.

What we did is this: We skated the first half of the middle circle. Then we skated the entire third circle. This was followed by the second half of the center circle. Passing from here, we then traced the entire lower circle, ending up where we started on the short axis between circles 1 and 2.

Just remember, one-half circle, full circle, one-half circle and full circle, shifting from right outside edge to right inside edge to left inside edge to left outside edge. There is nothing here that you have not done before. You just do them at different places.

Points you should watch are maintaining the correct edge to stay directly on the lines. Watch proper placement of your free leg to maintain balance so you will not be thrown off the line. Watch the positions of your arms and the way you hold your shoulders and body. If you find yourself going off the line in the beginning, experiment with different placements of your arms, shoulders and the way you lean.

Continue these experiments in body placement until you work out the combinations.
This is when you are working alone for the fun
of it. If you are headed for serious competition,
then you need a coach. It is his job to point
out the errors and tell you how to correct them.

Skating Backward

Skating backward sounds like an impossibil-
ity to a harassed beginner who is having difficulty just standing up on a pair of skates. But
once you learn to balance yourself on wheels
and can skate forward with some measure of

It is a good idea to get some help for your first effort at backward
skating. The instructor should face the student and hold her or his
hands for support.

grace, you can learn to skate backward without difficulty. The mechanics of backward skating are the same as for forward skating. You just do them backward.

Backward skating is most valuable and necessary in figure skating, dancing on skates, and in exhibition performances. In ordinary skating you don't really have to learn it, but it is a valuable trick to know, and can add variety to your fun skating.

You will remember that in forward skating we keep our body weight forward on the ball of the foot. In backward skating the average beginner automatically shifts weight to his heels. This is wrong and will unbalance you. Keep your weight forward.

You still work with a carrying leg on which you will roll and a pushing leg to give you the force to move.

It would be well to make your first backward pushes with a skating mate to support you through the first awkwardness of pushing in reverse.

One way this can be done is for the two of you to stand facing each other. Extend your arms. The instructor places his supporting hands under the beginner's elbows, and the beginner grasps the instructor's arms at a point on the inside of the elbow. This gives strong support in case of a fall. If such strong support is not needed, it may only be necessary to hold hands to help give initial balance.

The Reverse Shove

Here is the step-by-step procedure for skating backward:

1. Stand with knees slightly flexed with weight forward on the balls of your feet.

2. Have your feet together, ankle-to-ankle, and just far enough apart that they will not rub when you go into action.

3. If the right foot is your carrying foot, have it slightly flexed at the knee. It is rare that your skating foot is ever straight. This slight bending in effect makes your pushing foot longer in relation to your carrying foot. This permits a longer push for more starting and pushing power. The flexed knee also serves as a spring or shock absorber, as well as helping maintain balance.

4. Push *forward* and slightly to the side with the pushing foot to start rolling in reverse.

5. Then it is merely a matter of bringing the free leg down to become the carrying leg and pushing away with what had been the carrying leg. No difference from skating forward, except it is done in reverse.

The Difficult Part

Instructors have their own ways of doing things, and often they do not agree with each other. However, on backward skating they pretty well agree that the only difficult part of it lies in the mind of the beginning skater.

Backward skating employs the same technique as forward skating. However, you work in reverse. Here a skater is giving a forward shove with her pushing foot and rolling backward on her carrying foot. Keep your head turned to the side to see where you are going as much as possible.

By this time the beginner has fallen enough so that he is not particularly afraid of taking a tumble, but he is afraid of running into something. This causes tenseness. Tenseness leads to stiffness. Stiffness causes poor control and poor balance. When this happens the skater is headed for a fall.

This tenseness comes because you cannot see where you are going. It is not natural to proceed blindly. Even if you practice on an absolutely empty rink floor, there is still an uneasiness about skating backward for the first few times.

Under no circumstances should a skater go backward when skating on a street or sidewalk. You never know when something or someone will dart out unseen in back of you. Backward skating should be confined to exhibition skating.

In skating backward, skate with your head turned to one side. This will help you see partially where you are going. You will still have a blind side, however.

Advanced Figures

Once you have mastered skating forward and backward, you are ready to go on to more advanced figures. These we will not cover in this beginners' manual. However, just for familiarization and to show what you can go on to study, here is a brief description of some things that could lie ahead for you.

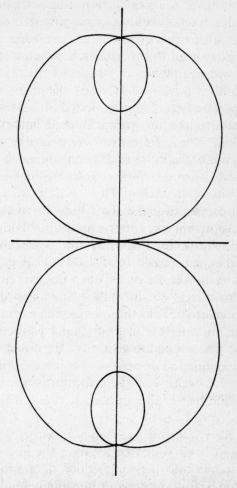

This is the basic pattern for the loop figure. The long axis runs straight through the loops. You enter the loops at the apexes.

One is a backward Circle 8 (ROB-LOB), school figure number 3. Here you start off on the short axis of the twin-circle pattern, skating backward to the left on an outside edge. You turn your head to the side so that you can see the trace to follow.

Another advanced figure is the ROF-LOF Loop. The basic figure is skated on a twin-circle pattern like the original Circle 8 figures you learned. The difference is that at the apex points of both circles (that is, the opposite ends of the two circles) there is an extra small inside loop on both circles. This small extra circle requires you to make some very sharp curves to stay within the pattern lines for this figure.

The basic ROF-LOF Loop is begun the same as your basic ROF-LOF. That is, you start at the short axis between the two circles, skating a right outside edge going forward. On the regular ROF-LOF you tried to get as much speed as possible in your initial pushoff because you wanted to go around the circle without wobbling. You still want to do that, if you can. But because of the sharp turns necessary to make the small loop circle, you don't want a fast speed.

Keep your free leg behind your employed leg and have your free leg over the line when you come into the loop. Your right shoulder should be low. Keep your free foot behind until you come to the top of the loop. Then bring your free foot forward. Watch the balance of

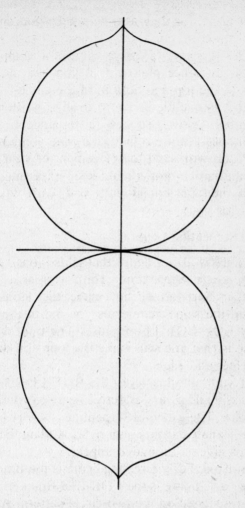

This is the basic pattern for the bracket figure.

your arms, for they also help keep you on the small trace.

This is a very effective figure, for it appears to the audience almost as if you had made a spin at the top and bottom of the circles.

This is a difficult figure to give written instruction about. Success is dependent upon your speed (not too fast), the edge you go into the loop with, and the placement of your free leg and arms. You should keep experimenting with their placement until you learn what is best for you.

The Serpentine Loop

There is also a figure that adds loops to the three-circle Serpentine. Here you skate the regular Serpentine, but make the loops, in much the same manner as you did in the regular ROF-LOF Loop figure. The only difference is that you will make the loops on different feet and edges.

If you have mastered the ROF-LOF Loop, you will add a very effective figure to your repertoire. The weaving Serpentine is a very beautiful maneuver in its own right. Adding the two loops gives it an added appeal.

Still another interesting figure is the Bracket. The basic figure is the LOB-LIB Bracket. This is also skated on the two-circle pattern. At the upper and lower apex points, instead of going inside the circle to make a loop, you curve slightly outward, change feet and take the same slight curve back to the basic circle again. This creates a small tip like the center of a punctuation bracket.

Many Figures

Since this is not a book on figure skating, we cannot go into all the different kinds there are. I think there are about sixty in all. Only about twenty-two of these are used in competitions, and even then you are only called upon to do four in competition. However, you do not know until you get your instructions what these four will be.

The requirements in competition vary with the different divisions. These are senior, junior and—if it is a local competition—sometimes a beginners or novice division. But while the figures chosen may vary with the different divisions, they will be the same for all skaters within a division.

In learning figure skating, you really need an instructor—or at least someone who knows figures—to coach and point out your errors. You can't see yourself and sometimes the trouble you may be having is simply the wrong placement of a free leg, the improper movement of your hands, too much or too little pushoff speed and the like.

In competition skating, the school figures are just half of your presentation. You will also have to do a freestyle routine before you can take home a medal or trophy.

CHAPTER 7

FREESTYLE AND EXHIBITIONS

In freestyle figure skating a contestant gets to present his or her own program. Here you are judged upon your skating ability, the program that you present (content) and your originality. In regular competitions, you can't get too far out with your content, but in special competition devoted solely to freestyle, the sky is the limit.

Certainly an outstanding freestyle show is the Gold Skate Classic, held in Bakersfield, California. It is purely an amateur show, drawing entrants from clubs around the country, but the costuming and execution are comparable to top show business anywhere.

This is natural enough, since showmanship is one of the things contestants are judged on. Each act is developed around a theme and how you interpret that theme is also noted in the judging. Costumes and, of course, skating ability are other points the judges consider in awarding the top places.

The Freestyle Content

A winning freestyle content (repertoire) is not just assembling a lot of things you have seen other skaters do. You must have some originality in your act if you hope to win. This difference may be a new combination of old things. Or it may be in a different and interpretive footwork that you employ. It is no good to be just like the rest, even if you are a little better than the rest. The other skater will win if he is more original.

The key here is originality and difference. You will be judged on how difficult your routines are, but just being hard is not the key to success. Showmanship and surprises for judges and audiences are more important than purely difficult technical performances. However, if you can combine all of these things into one program, then you are really out in front of the pack.

In any event, your program should be planned for four to five minutes. You will be given a time in competition and are expected to stay within ten seconds or so of it. You can lose points by being too short or too long.

Ordinarily a figure-skating program for serious competition is put together by the skater's instructor or coach. This is okay, for coaches

Fancy footwork pays off in freestyle skating. You can practice it anywhere, even while out rolling on a skate path in the park.

A group of skaters practicing freestyle show different types of footwork.

are generally ex-champions themselves. They know what will appeal to judges.

But if you are all alone, then it is up to you to work out your own program. I talked to several skaters who began by themselves before they could interest a really good coach in taking them on for training for the big time.

"I started out," one said, "by watching and copying the good boys and girls. I know that this doesn't get you first-place awards. It lacks originality. But I wasn't after medals then. I was trying to learn how. Once I learned their way of doing things, then I started looking around for ways to improve and change the things I had learned.

"After all, there are only so many different ways you can roll around on skates. Everybody rolls forward, curves, spins, jumps and rolls backward. After that it is primarily a matter of rearranging these old standbys to make your program look different.

"Also on those things that I kept from basic routines, I tried to do better than my competitors. Could I add a little something that would make it different? For example, if he or she does a double jump, what can I do? I am not able to expand this by doing a triple jump, but could I possibly do a double jump and then come down in a split?

"Maybe and maybe not, but let me try and see if I can thus top the other comedians' gags. You take everything any of them do and give

Good freestyle means adding some new touch to skating routines by rearranging old standbys to make your program look different. In working out his skate dance, this skater uses music from headphone radios to help his rhythm.

it this acid test: Can I do it better and just a little differently? If you apply this philosophy to everything you want to add to your content, then you are well on the road to becoming a really original skater. While originality is not the only thing you are graded on, it really helps.''

Another Voice Heard From

Another freestyle expert had this advice to pass along to a beginner trying to work out his own content: "Pace yourself. You have been told that the more difficult and original your content is, the better chance you have of winning. I heard that, too. So I broke my neck trying to make everything hard. What this did was wear me out so that I finished up my program worn out and limp as a rag. The final routines suffered because of it.

"That's when I learned to pace myself. You don't have to make every figure a triple somersault in the air. You are not a circus clown.

"So pace yourself. Set up a less physically demanding part before you go into your really man-killing show-stopper. This should not be something so easy that it is obvious. Maybe it could be some novel and tricky footwork that will take the judges' and audience's minds off the fact that you are catching your breath to gather steam to really sock it to them.''

Still another had this tip for beginners: "In the beginning I thought I had to get out there and dazzle them with speed and bang-bang action. It didn't get me anywhere. Then I awoke to what is called 'contrast.' Sometimes an artist will want to make a color look more vivid than his paint will allow. He can actually make his reddest red look redder by placing it beside his most vivid green.

"You can do the same thing in freestyle skating. If you have a routine that calls for dazzling speed of execution for effect, you can make it appear faster by preceding it with a slow, graceful set of movements."

Work for Other Contrasts

While he did not say so, you could do well to work for other types of contrast as well. Make each unit of your content as much different from the other as the format of the competition will permit you to do.

If you have seen your competitors, then you will want to make your content a contrast to theirs. If we watch a string of contestants do pretty much the same thing one after another, then it is really refreshing to have the next skater come out and give us an entirely different show.

If this is a competition like Golden Skate, where lighting, costuming, and music are part of the judging, then you want to make these as original as possible.

If you want to work out your own content and routines, then you really have to be more than a skater. You must be director, stage manager and stage electrician all rolled into one. It also helps if you know something about dance choreography.

And on top of that, some lessons in ballet dancing are the best possible grounding you can get for figure and freestyle skating. Ballet is the very personification of grace in movement, and that is a basic foundation of winning freestyle and figure skating as well.

A Final Word on Freestyle

In putting together your content, you are well advised to work the way a writer does. That is, build up to a climax. Don't present your show-stopper first and then have your program go down in interest the rest of the time.

Build up to your best feat gradually, so there is a continual rising of interest right up to your smashing climax in which the hero (you, of course) brings down the house with cheers and applause (let us *hope*).

The experts all emphasized the need for constant practice. This means practicing school and freestyle figures. Except for learning to balance yourself on skates, they agreed that street skating is not sufficient practice.

Dance training is a great help in working out routines for your freestyle content. It is not just girls, but boys as well, who can benefit from dance training as a background for skating competition.

Dancing on Skates

Dancing on skates is a sort of combination between figure, freestyle and exhibition skating today. At one time the most popular roller-skating dance styles were the regular ballroom waltz, fox trot and tango, and skated by a man and woman team. The dances were very stylized and based upon short gliding strokes by the two principals. These dances are pretty and, if done correctly, often are poems in grace.

However, they are slow for modern tastes, and the current rage is for disco dancing on roller skates. Here is something right up to the minute in modernity. While dancing fads come and go—who today remembers the Charleston and the Big Apple?—it is quite possible that disco dancing will survive as a modern dance form.

Disco dancing is definitely advanced roller skating. You had better know how to keep from falling no matter how your body twists and turns. Once you have mastered this, then you should attend a dancing school to learn disco dancing without skates. After that, you can modify the steps and routines to fit your roller-skating technique. A thorough mastery of figure and freestyle skating will be a help in moving into disco land.

Speed Skating

Speed skating is the most exciting of the competitive skating sports. While there is excitement, of course, in figure competition, only one person competes at a time. You never know who is winning until the judges announce their decisions.

But in speed skating the contestants line up in old-fashioned, man-against-man style and

Dancing on skates is becoming increasingly popular, spreading into the new disco dancing fad.

struggle to get around the banked track ahead of the pack.

Speed skating is a tough grind. Speed skaters hit around 20 miles per hour. In addition they are constantly maneuvering in and out of tight spots. This calls for a remarkable reserve of energy. If you don't have stamina, speed skating is not for you. Although skaters go around in a rectangle with all left turns, they still have to be expert in skating on all edges to take care of the constant ins and outs.

The Speed Track

The track is laid out inside a rectangle with four small pylons in each corner. These are for the skaters to turn around. There is a "pylon judge" at each of these points to make sure that the skaters go around the markers and do not shave inches by cutting inside. They also watch for fouls and blocking. Blocking is weaving in front of a skater to prevent him from going around you.

The start is at the center left side and the skaters go counterclockwise around the track. The distance skated varies with the event. Some events are five miles, two miles and one mile. Also there are 880-yard and 440-yard events as well. Young skaters do not have to race so far. There are one-sixteenth-mile and one-half-mile events in the junior division.

On a five-mile run you can make a poor start and recover—if you are good enough. But in the short races, the skater who gets off the line first has a decided advantage.

Speed Track Skates

Special skates are used in speed skating. Every effort is made to make them lighter than other skates. Wooden wheels are used. Formerly these were of maple, but in recent years manufacturers have turned to sycamore and pine. These wooden wheels grip well and are lighter than other wheels. Also holes have been bored in the skate plates. This cuts down weight.

This may seem like a small amount of weight and beginners often wonder how much good it does to shave off a few ounces. The answer is that it takes energy and strength to move anything. The less you have to move, the more of your energy—you only have so much—goes into moving fast. And moving fast is what speed skating is all about. You may have to go around that indoor track sixteen times and every ounce you can shed is going to help you in the end.

Precision bearings are preferred in other types of skating, but are controversial in speed skating. Some skaters prefer the open bearings, believing that they give less friction and

This is a staged shot from the film <u>Kansas City Bomber</u>, made by MGM, but it gives a good picture of the type of pileups that delighted Roller Derby fans. (From the MGM release KANSAS CITY BOMBER © 1972 Metro-Goldwyn-Mayer Inc.)

a faster takeoff. It could be that the preference is just opinion and that the advantages of one type over the other balance out over the entire race.

Roller Derby

The Roller Derby is probably the best known skating activity. It has had vast television coverage over the years and has drawn enormous crowds during its traveling tours.

The Roller Derby and competing organizations that have sprung up are spectator sports. They are pure exhibitions. The name Roller

Derby was invented and copyrighted by Leo Seltzer. The name cannot be used by anyone else. Roller Derby, being a trademark, is always spelled with capital letters. It is incorrect—and illegal—to call any similar show a Roller Derby.

Seltzer originated the idea for the Roller Derby in Chicago in 1935. He had been running a string of theaters during the 1920s, but the Depression wiped these out. He turned to live show exhibitions and promotions.

Then in 1935 someone told him that a magazine article claimed that ninety-three percent of all people in the United States had roller skated at some time in their lives.

An Idea Is Born

They were sitting at a restaurant table when his friend informed Seltzer of the skating article. An idea immediately clicked. If ninety-three percent of the people knew about skating, there should be enough interest left in them to pull an audience into a really spectacular skating show. The Roller Derby legend claims he ruined the table cloth by scribbling out a track design and some rough rules on the cloth.

He first considered an endurance exhibition. This would be patterned after the then popular marathon dancing shows. Today's youth will recall the marathon dancers from the hit movie

They Shoot Horses, Don't They? in which Jane Fonda starred. Couples danced with short breaks until they dropped with exhaustion. The only rewards were small prizes.

He finally settled on the idea of a transcontinental race held in the Chicago Coliseum. The circular track was one fourteenth of a mile and skaters had to make 57,000 laps to supposedly equal the more than 4,000-mile distance from San Diego, California to New York. A huge score board in the form of a map of the United States had markers to show the audiences the progress of each skater in the long grind from California to the East Coast.

The original Derby teams consisted of a man and a woman skater. They did not roll together, but alternated. There were cots where they could get a little sleep between rolls on the track. They were fed, but got nothing else except a chance to win the $1000 prize.

On the average the skaters "moved their markers" 110 miles a day. This made each skater have to average 55 miles a day, with the skating sessions running from 1:30 in the afternoon to 12:30 that night.

For the record, the winning team was Bernard McKay and Corrisse Martin.

Derbies on Tour

The crowds packed the place and Seltzer decided to take the show on tour to other major cities. It did well at first, but interest waned. Seltzer changed his format and moved more toward the showmanship idea of professional wrestling. Shorter races were set up and skaters, now on small salaries, were encouraged to get rough with each other.

This perked up interest again and the Roller Derby was off to a fabulous future, spurred by the rise of television in the late 1940s.

As the Roller Derby shook down, two teams of five skaters each took the track. Only two members of each team could score. They were called jammers and wore striped helmets. The rest of the team was supposed to block the opponents and let the jammers race ahead. Points were awarded for racing ahead, circling the track, and lapping (that is, going a full turn or lap of the track ahead of one's opponents). One point was awarded for each opponent lapped.

Roller Derbies got pretty rough at times, but that was what the fans came to see.

The Roller Derby enjoyed great favor for a while and then went into an eclipse. It came roaring back in the early 1970s, pulling in thousands of spectators. Then interest dropped again, but with Roller Derby's history of ups and downs, who can say that it will not be packing the rinks again soon?

CHAPTER 8

FUN ON SKATES

We have talked a lot about getting started with its hard work and bumps, competition figure skating with its grueling practice and speed skating with its tough grind. All of these require hard work, which you may enjoy, but it is work.

For those among us who are not overly fond of work, there is a lot roller skating can offer us in the way of just pure fun with no competitive pressure.

On the fun side of skating there is just going for a rolling stroll, gliding along as if you had wings on your feet.

If you want something a little more challenging, you might try a slalom course. This is a roller-skating takeoff from the popular skiing zig-zag around fixed markers on a downhill course.

The Slalom

A slalom course can be set up anywhere there is a free downhill area. Plastic markers are set up about five feet apart. Sometimes, if the runners want to make it hard on themselves, they can be much closer than this. In Venice, California, there is a seaside park where skaters, skateboarders, bicyclists and pedestrians gather in mobs on weekends and holidays. A semipermanent slalom is set up in front of the auditorium in the mornings. It is nothing more than a straight line of empty soft drink cans.

The cans work fine. They are easily knocked aside if a skater hits one. And if you fall on one, they are soft aluminum and the can crushes before you do.

There is an unwritten rule that everyone observes: If you knock down a can, you come back and put it in place again. The cans sit there all day. Any skater or skateboard rider can come along and try his or her skill whenever he or she feels like it. And it is busy the whole day long.

Good Practice

In addition to being fun in itself, the slalom course is good practice in leaning and making edges as you cut left on one can and then back right to weave around the other. Both freestyle

LEFT: Two skaters on a slalom run demonstrate right and left turns. The boy is making a right turn on the outside edge of his foot. The girl in front is halfway around a left outside edge turn. Note the lean of their bodies and the use of their arms for balance in making the sharp one-foot turns.

TOP RIGHT: Here is an example of fancy footwork in riding the slalom course.

BOTTOM RIGHT: A couple doubleup for a back wheel tandem descent of the slalom run.

A slalom course is good practice in learning to lean properly to make curves.

skaters and roller-hockey players can ride the slalom course to their foot-training advantage.

In riding the course, you take a running start, building up the speed you need, and then coast through the markers. You may ride on two feet, one foot, or criss-cross them, as I saw one skater do. He crossed his legs at the knees, making a V-shaped opening between the lower parts of his legs. He straddled the cans in his weaving instead of going around them. This was an unusual touch that brought a round of applause from those watching. As experienced skaters themselves, they appreciated seeing someone add a neat touch, going a little beyond what the rest were doing.

The technique of slalom riding is nothing that requires any new knowledge. All you are doing is making right and left curves. You may be making them more sharply than you have been required to do before, however.

Since the markers for a slalom are set up on an incline, a good way to begin, if you have never done this before, is to skip the running

Take it easy on your first slalom rolls. Just coast slowly down the incline until you can make your curves correctly.

start. Just roll up to the first can and let the incline roll you gently downhill, making sharp right and left curves around the cans.

The idea is to get the feel of things through a slow action. Then gradually speed up as you gain experience and confidence. Too many slalom beginners try to go too fast in the beginning.

Once you master the back and forth shift on two feet, you begin on other variations. Try a one-foot slalom, first on the right foot and then on the left. Try crossing your feet and coming down that way. I saw one skater throw in a novelty by spiraling around each can. He came down in a corkscrew pattern instead of the usual wave motion. Like any other skating routine, there is great opportunity for variations. All it takes is a little imagination—and some skating ability, of course.

Roller-Skate Acrobatics

If you have taken gymnastic training, as we advised in talking about roller-skating safety, then you may be able to work out some pleasing skating acrobatics.

Spins, jumps, somersaults in the air and even back flips are not difficult for those with proper training.

There is a neat trick called "shooting the

This is a basic pattern for a simple slalom course.

duck,'' which can be done without the risk that more advanced acrobatics require.

In this maneuver you crouch down on one leg as you skate ahead. Then you extend the free leg straight out in front of you.

In the beginning, it is necessary for you to use your hands and arms to get the leg out and support it in the air. After some practice, you should be able to get that foot out without support.

Then you can add variations like throwing in a spin at the end of the roll.

Kicking the Puck Around

Since roller skates originated as a substitute for ice skates, it was inevitable that sooner or

"Shooting the duck" is skating in a one-foot crouch while extending the other foot directly in front. Normally the toe would be pointed up, but in this picture the skater is coming around in a spin for a more dramatic ending for a straight roll.

later someone would try to play hockey on skates.

The name hockey comes from *hoquet,* a French word for a shepherd's crook, and refers to the bent stick used in hockey. The game is very old. A tomb carving in the Athens museum shows boys playing hockey 2500 years ago.

Roller hockey started as a street game in New York in the 1920s. It continued as a street game until the first roller hockey rink was built in Brooklyn in the 1960s. Since then interest in the sport has grown in the northeastern section of the country.

The spread of regular ice hockey to other sections of the country (there are even professional teams in California now) has spurred interest in roller hockey.

Away from the Northeast the interest is mainly in half-court hockey because of lack of rinks to play in. Half-court hockey squeezes the game into a smaller area, with both teams using the same goal. Its advantage is that it can be played in a 60- × 80-foot area or even smaller.

Players can use the same goal by juggling the rules a bit. This permits the defenders to become the attackers by getting the puck outside a marked playing area.

The Game

Hockey is played on a rectangular court. It begins with two players, who compare to the centers in basketball, who "face off" in the center of the court. The referee tosses the puck, a rubber doughnut-shaped disk, in between them. Each player tries to tip the puck toward his side. Then it is just a matter of each side trying to knock the puck into their goal cage. An opposing goal tender—"goalie"— stands in front of each cage, at opposite ends of the court, to keep the opposing team from slapping in the puck for a score.

That is all there is to it, except for the details, and it would take a book to go into all of them. Generally, the team pushing the puck finds the opposing team trying to block or take the puck away from them. This often leads to quite a bit of roughness, for hockey players, both on ice and on roller skates, are a pugnacious group. Rules on sportsmanship don't mean a lot to these hardy souls.

That is why the penalty box is an integral part of any hockey game.

The Penalty Box

The penalty box is the "jail" where rule breakers go. You get sent to the penalty box for such things as butt ending (sticking the end of your hockey stick into an opponent), elbowing, hooking (tripping an opponent with the bent end of your stick) and similar misdemeanors. Minor penalties draw two minutes in the box and major penalties draw three minutes. During this time, the team has to play without you. This can be quite a handicap if the opposing team is strong.

Hockey fields six players to a side. Sometimes half-court roller hockey cuts the players to three or four to a side to keep from jamming up small courts.

The regulation team has a center, left and right wing men, right and left defense men and the goalie.

Clothing

No type of hockey should be played without proper protective clothing. A helmet is a must, and you would be wise to add a mouth guard. Pucks don't just scoot across the rink. They often take off in flight. Hockey sticks are swinging wildly, and spills are common.

In addition to the helmet, your body needs padding. There is a lot of body contact in hockey. So use hip pads, elbow guards, a cup under your pants, and shin guards.

If you are the goalie, then you need additional protective clothing. This includes a baseball-type chest protector, heavy leg guards, full face mask, a huge block glove to knock down pucks by hand, shoulder pads and a hockey stick with a wider blade than the rest of the team.

Skating in Roller Hockey

In this sport a skater has to be able to make sharp and sudden turns. You can't glide on concrete like an ice skater can on his frozen rink. So a roller-hockey player has to work harder than an ice skater does.

Interest in roller hockey is growing. If none is played in your locality, you might talk to the local parks and recreation people about starting some teams. As a general rule, you can take any of the numerous books on ice hockey and adapt their rules and advice to roller hockey.

Can Jumping

A skating stunt that you see quite often where skaters gather in parks is can jumping. This is another stunt borrowed from ice skaters who jump over wooden barrels. Since wooden barrels are not as common as they once were, skaters line up metal trash cans and jump over them.

This is definitely post-graduate roller skating and not recommended for a beginner. If you do want to take up jumping, it is best to begin with short hops, wearing all the protective clothing you can put on.

The secret is landing correctly. This means with feet together so that you land on both at the same time. Still keep your weight forward on the balls of your feet and use your body balance to keep upright as you land.

Jumping over a row of trash cans is a spectacular stunt, but it can be a dangerous one. Note that the jumper is keeping his feet together. He will land on his front wheels with his rump well back to counteract the natural tendency of his body to go forward over the wheels when he lands.

Just remember that there is no sand pit for you to land in as there is for broad jumpers. You are going to sit yourself down on concrete.

It might be well to start with jumping over cardboard boxes. Then if you fall short, you will fall on something collapsible and not hard metal.

CHAPTER 9

SKATE CARE

There are a number of different makes of skates. They range from plastic models for young children to expensive imported rink, figure and speed skates for serious competition or professional use. No one agrees upon which is the best. Each make has its supporters who swear by them.

Your best bet is to talk to the pro at a skating rink. He has had a lot of experience and can give you the best advice.

But although nobody agrees upon the best skates, everyone agrees that your skates will be no better than the care you give them. There are perfectionists like some speed skaters who claim that just one grain of dust working its way into a sealed bearing will produce enough friction to slow a skater down sufficiently to make a difference in a closely matched race.

Few will go to that extreme, but skate care

is important, if for no other reason than that you will invest quite a bit in a really good pair of boot skates. You should take care of them to protect your investment.

Safety is involved also. You can get hurt on poorly maintained equipment.

Pre-Roll Shakedown

Just as a pilot preflights his airplane before taking off, you should give your skates a pre-roll shakedown also.

First, let's give the skates a good eyeballing where the action is. We'll begin by making sure that the boot sole is still fastened securely to the skate plate. They don't come loose often, but it can be disastrous when they do.

If you are still using one of the oldtime clamp-on skates, then check the clamps for cracks. Be sure the clamp screw is not worn or loose—and stays in place when you screw it down to tighten the right and left toe clamp around your shoe sole. The strap and buckle, which come around your ankle, should get some attention. Leather gets worn or rotten on these older skates. You don't want it giving way on you. It could cause you a badly twisted ankle.

Next, take a look at the skate plate. Are all the rivets still secure and any bolts still tight? Look for cracks in the metal. If you are going in for strenuous skating where the skates take a lot of punishment, this is especially important.

The Trucks

There are two trucks, fore and aft. They are pretty much alike, except for the necessary differences because of their front and back positions. The truck, as we mentioned earlier, is the assembly that holds the wheels in position and which controls the action of the wheels.

The base of the truck is a triangular piece of metal. There is a hole at one end. The axle for the wheels goes through the broad end. A tapering spur rises from this to form the pivot which is joined to the base plate by a rubber grommet. The pivot will permit a small amount of movement to aid in leaning the skate. On the opposite side (this would be on the inside of the front truck) another spur holds a large metal washer-like piece. This forms the center support for the cushion, on a double-action cushion. An action-adjusting bolt goes through the cushions and their supports and screws into an action-adjusting bolt lock-nut.

Adjusting the Cushions

The bolt that goes through the rubber bushings (the cushions) has a screwdriver slot in the top end (as viewed from the bottom of the skate). The opposite end has the action-adjusting bolt lock-nut, mentioned above.

The amount the rubber cushions can be compressed determines the amount of curve a skate will take when the skater leans to one side or the other. The amount of compression can be adjusted by tightening the bolt (sometimes called a king pin) that runs through the cushion assembly.

This adjustment is made by turning the slot in the bolt end. A large screwdriver is used. This screws or unscrews the bolt's threaded end into the action-adjusting bolt nut.

How much to adjust the "action" depends upon the weight of a skater, how he or she

Tightening the adjustments on the cushions will change the action of the skate.

leans, and sometimes upon the age of the rubber spacers. Rubber loses some of its bounce when it ages.

A loose truck responds more easily to body lean. A tight truck is more stable. Beginners will do better with a tight truck. It is less likely to make movements that you do not expect and certainly don't want. A tighter truck is also used in figure skating for more precise control of the circles.

Beginners are advised to start with a tight truck—but not so tight that you can't compress it. As you learn control, you can loosen up for improved maneuverability.

Checking Wheels and Bearings

Wheels were originally made of wood or metal. Wooden wheels are still preferred by some speed skaters. Then about fifteen years ago a tough plastic called polyurethane came into use and now has been adapted for skate wheels. Polyurethane has a soft, soapy look about it. It can be made in either a soft or a hard wheel.

The soft polyurethane wheel was the first on the market. It was great for outdoor skating, but too slippery on hard rink floors. Now you can get a harder polyurethane wheel that is a sure gripper on the rink's epoxy-coated floors.

Polyurethane does not crack like wood. So

Spinning the wheels will let you test for worn or binding bearings, wheel wobble and worn tread.

a wheel inspection is more concerned with how freely the wheel turns on its bearings and the wear condition of the wheel surfaces.

Spin your wheels to see how free-wheeling they are. The wheel bearings are steel balls that fit around the axle to permit the wheel to turn with a minimum of friction. But poor lubrication or dirt in the bearings can cause them to bind. Sealed bearings are not supposed to give trouble, but it does happen. In that case, bearings must be removed for cleaning and re-lubrication.

Also, watch for wheel wobble. This may indicate wear in the bearings or axle shaft. Or the lock-nuts that hold the wheel to the axle might be loose.

Always check the polyurethane tread. So much curve riding—it is rare that a skater trav-

Check for wear. This toestop has been worn down. It does not need to be replaced yet, but it soon will be.

els in an exactly straight line—may cause one side of the wheel to wear more than the other. It is a simple matter to remove the lock-nuts and rotate the wheels for longer life. Also, check your toestops for wear, just as you would check the brakes on a car.

Things to Avoid

One of the best preventive medicines for skates is to be careful where you do your rolling. Wet pavement should be avoided because it is often slippery. Worse for skates is that water often collects in puddles on sidewalks and skate paths. Some skaters like to plow through these to watch the water spray.

This is one of the worst things you can do to a pair of skates. The water will work itself into your bearings and cause rust. You will need to clean them thoroughly after a water bath. If rust does get into the bearings, about the only thing you can do is replace them.

Sand is also bad for skates. In beach or other sandy areas, the wind often piles sand up on the skate paths. If this gets into your bearings or axle shafts, it works exactly like sandpaper. You'll soon be buying new bearings, wheels or trucks.

Caring for Your Boots

Your skating boots should be given the same care you would give a fine pair of shoes. You don't have to roll through water to get your skate boots wet. Perspiration can do it too. Dry them out. Putting damp boots back in a dark closet may, in some climates, cause them to mold or mildew. They should be dried in a well-ventilated place away from heat.

And *do* use shoe trees to keep your skate boots in shape.

CHAPTER 10

SKATEBOARDS

Riding a skateboard is a form of skating, for the board is just an enlarged skate itself. Although the board (corresponding to the plate in a roller skate) is big enough for two feet to ride on, the undercarriage is our familiar polyurethane wheels riding on roller-skate trucks. You can swap wheels on your skateboard and roller skates, if you wish, for they are identical.

The boom in skateboarding came about because of the development of polyurethane wheels. Skateboarding first became popular in the 1960s, but the wheels then in use were dangerous and the boom quickly died out.

Then the switch to polyurethane wheels revived interest in skateboarding. Polyurethane's non-skid qualities cause the wheels to grip the pavement. There are fewer accidents now. Formerly the board would slip too easily from under a rider. In addition, the gripping quality of polyurethane permits spectacular stunts that were impossible on the old skateboards. Visit any skateboard park and you will see some fantastic riding stunts.

How to Ride a Skateboard

Riding the skateboard is different from riding skates, but there are enough similarities that a good skater will have no trouble picking up the differences very quickly.

As in roller skating, the main thing is balance. If you can balance skates, you can balance a skateboard. Skateboards are not as solid a platform as skates are. They do some wobbling that you must get used to.

You still use the action of the truck to guide the board. That is, like skating, it is all in the leaning.

A beginner on skateboarding is advised to have a partner support him for his first roll out on the board. However, if one is adding skateboarding after learning roller skating, then it is much easier to begin alone.

The first thing to do is to "dry run" the board. That is, learn to stand on it without moving. In this way you can perhaps become accustomed to the unsteadiness of the board as compared to your roller skates.

You also practice leaning to get the different feel of the skateboard.

The First Takeoff

1. Your carrying foot is placed on the board about midway between the front and back truck. Your knee is bent perhaps a little more than in a roller skating pushoff. This is because you need more push on your pushing foot. You will need to lean your body forward at the

You can see some fantastic stunts in a skateboard park. Here a skateboarder defies gravity in swinging his way up and down a half-circular concrete pipe.

waist. This is to counteract any loss of balance when you push off. A few experimental push-offs will show you how much forward lean is necessary for your size and weight. Remember, this lean is *forward*. Any side leans will cause an edge that will have you traveling in circles.

2. The next step is much like riding a scooter.

If you have any trouble with your first skateboard ride, roll beside a rail where you can use one hand to support yourself.

Bring your pushing foot down on the pavement near the nose of the skateboard. Push back with it to roll the board—and yourself, hopefully—forward. We say hopefully because a lot of skaters taking up skateboarding for the first time think they are still on skates.

As a result, they try to start too fast. A fast start can and often should be made. However, one who is unfamiliar with a skateboard's peculiarities can kick the board right out from under himself. So take it easy on the first few rides. Push gently until you understand the effect the board is going to have on your balance. Then as you gain experience and confidence, you can get a little wilder in your takeoffs.

3. Your weight is on your pushing foot during the takeoff push. Make your one push and shift weight to your riding (carrying) foot. Bring your pushing foot up on the board behind your carrying foot and coast along. One push-off is enough until you get the feel of the board, and can control it with confidence.

Riding Foot Positions

There are two basic positions for your feet when riding (coasting) on a skateboard. Regardless of the style you choose, in the beginning place your feet so they are balanced between the two trucks. Later you can get fancy with your footwork and even "hang ten"—that is, place your feet so far forward that your toes hang over the edge, a gimmick taken from surfing.

One basic foot position is the "regular foot." The other is the "goofy foot." The only difference is the foot that you put forward. The left foot is in front on the regular foot ride. Some say you can make right body turns easier

This young woman is riding regular foot with her left foot out in front.

with it. The goofy foot ride reverses things. You ride with your right foot forward.

It doesn't make a lot of difference either way. You'll find regular-footed and goofy-footed champions. It all comes down to which way is most comfortable for you.

After you learn to balance yourself while coasting after the single push, you are ready to start adding new things. The first thing will be

This young woman is riding the goofy foot style. That is, she has her right foot forward, instead of the left foot forward for the regular foot style.

continued pushes. Push off, put the pushing foot on the board and coast until you begin to slow down; push again, coast and push again, and coast some more.

How to Stop

One way is to step off the board. If you do so, remember to hit the ground running so you expend your momentum moving along.

Another way is to move your weight back and press down on the tail of the board until it drags. You have to watch your balance here, for the front wheels come up in a wheelie. This sort of thing is hard on skateboards.

Steering

Skateboards, because of the cushioned roller skate-type trucks, are steered exactly like skates. That is, lean your body in the direction you want the board to curve.

Some skateboards have a kicktail. This is an upcurving section at the back of the board. It permits your foot to remain flat while raising the nose for stops, wheelies and tricks. It is also a big help in making a one-eighty (a 180° turn).

To do the one-eighty, put your foot on the kicktail and press down to raise the front wheels off the pavement. Then use your free foot and arms to swing yourself around so that you are facing the direction you came from.

Take this easy at first, so that you don't swing yourself right off the board.

An endover is made by putting your feet on opposite ends of the board and flipping it around. Making an endover on the side of a pipe like this requires real skill.

Endovers and Wheelies

The one-eighty can be turned into a skateboard trick simply by repeating it. After you swing around, weight the other end and swing around again. Continue the reversals as long as you wish. This is called an endover.

The same technique you used to weight down the tail and drag it to a stop can be used for a wheelie. A wheelie is riding along on the back wheels with the front wheels in the air. For a two-foot wheelie, just don't weight the back enough to drag the tail.

A one-foot wheelie is done in much the same manner. Move the carrying foot to the tail and

This is a good example
of a front-end wheelie.

press down to bring the nose up. When you
have the back foot centered and balanced, lift
up the free foot and use it to help keep your
balance.

It is also possible to do nose wheelies. In
this trick, you weight the front end to raise the
tail.

Where to Go from Here

This has been only a very brief discussion of
the possibilities of skateboards as a supplement
to your regular roller skates. If you would like
to go into this exciting new sport more thoroughly, we can recommend *Skateboards and
Skateboarding* by La Vada Weir and published
by the same publishers as this book.

CHAPTER 11

WHERE TO SKATE

Skaters have been using sidewalks and roads for longer than any of us have been alive. Unfortunately, both are dangerous places to skate. The streets are banned because of traffic. Even less traveled residential streets should be avoided, for you never know when a car will pull out of a driveway or come scooting around a corner. A skater is hard to see.

Sidewalks are safer from traffic, but they are for pedestrians. The number of walkers who have been knocked down by skaters has justified many towns and cities in passing laws forbidding skating on sidewalks.

In the last few years a number of cities have been painting lines for exclusive bike paths along their streets. Skaters, however, are not welcome. In some parks you may skate along the sidewalks, but are still banned from the bike paths.

In many localities skaters are barred from bike paths. Be sure to ask about local rules and follow them.

Resort and vacation areas are more lenient. Some like Venice, California have the street facing the ocean blocked off for pedestrians, bicyclists, skateboarders, and—thank heaven—skaters. They still don't want you on the concrete bike paths and back up the prohibition with a fine if you are caught. There are other places along the California coast where the city fathers do not look with such disfavor on mixing bikes and skates. There is no evidence that bicyclists knock down any more skaters here than in places where the mix is banned.

168

The Skaters' Best Friend

If you live in one of those places that frown on sidewalk skating, then your friend in need is your friendly roller rink operator. And believe me, he is a true friend of all skaters. In many cases he will do more than just provide a rink for you to roll around in. He can be the open door that leads to the joys of competition skating and—who knows—maybe even a world championship in figure skating.

But if you don't want to go that far, he may sponsor many other events that make skating more than just rolling up and down the sidewalk.

Streets and sidewalks are no place for skaters. Go to a skating rink, a skateboard park or a public park where skaters are welcome.

The RSROA

The rink operator can be especially helpful to you if he is a member of RSROA—the Roller Skating Rink Operators Association. This organization was started in 1937 and since that time has done an extraordinary job in sponsoring skating activities.

These activities go beyond just local events in the members' own individual rinks. They sponsor national championships and international events as well. Their aim is to help spread roller skating, and this they certainly do.

The first national event RSROA sponsored was a speed skating championship meet in Cincinnati, Ohio, in 1938. This was so successful that the following year RSROA added a figure-skating championship event to its schedule. This was held in Detroit, and the first skate-dancing championship was held in Mineola, New York.

Then, in 1940, the speed races, figure-skating and roller-dancing events were combined in one meet for the first time. This was also in Cincinnati. It was the beginning of the events sponsored today by RSROA.

It was in 1941 that RSROA started an annual school to teach instructors and to establish rules for the different competitions. Instructors accredited by RSROA will have a card indicating this. This card means that RSROA has checked him or her out and that the instructor follows standard methods of teaching. Non-accredited instructors may be just as good as those who are accredited, but they are not likely to be any better. RSROA is jealous of its reputation and you have to be good to earn the association's endorsement.

Other Associations

The first skating association was organized by James L. Plimpton, the father of modern roller skating and inventor of the rocking skate that made roller skating popular. Plimpton made enough money selling skates to build a $100,000 roller rink in New York City. He then founded the New York Roller Skating Association to build interest in the new sport. Later he built another palatial rink in Newport, Rhode Island.

Plimpton also established what may be the first American award for skating. This was a certificate of merit. It entitled the winner to skate free in any of Plimpton's rinks.

Skating got another boost when the first six-day roller skate race was held in New York's Madison Square Garden. The top award went to a fast skater who rolled over 1,000 miles in his six days on the circular rink.

Then through the years skating had its ups and downs. The improvement of the bicycle and the invention of the automobile gave young sportsmen something else to occupy their interest. Roller skating made a comeback just before World War I, dropped in interest in the 1920s, and then was revived again in the Depression years of the 1930s.

The sport was further helped by formation of the Amateur Roller Skating Association, which was affiliated with the Amateur Athletic Union (AAU). Another rink operators' organization, the United Rink Operators (URO), was also formed.

Roller skating gained interest in the 1950s, had a setback in the 1960s, but now is enjoying another boom in popularity. As one rink operator put it, "Roller skating as a sport is just like a roller skater. It may take a fall now and then, but it gets back on its feet and rolls on better than ever."

Skating Has Come a Long Way

To see how far roller skating has come, you should drop in sometime to see the Golden Skate Classic, held each year in Bakersfield, California. It draws contestants from skating clubs throughout the West for a truly spectacular dance- and freestyle-skating exhibition.

Showmanship is as important as skating ability in this stunning presentation. You will see costumes and routines that will match any professional ice-skating show.

There are plenty of places to rent skates if you don't want to buy your own.

A Final Word

Roller skating is once again an "in" thing. More people are roller skating today than ever before. Skates have been improved and are safer now. Skating rinks are no longer big barns. Some have been decorated on theme designs, and the epoxy coverings used on the

Skateboard parks usually welcome roller skaters and provide unusual places to practice.

wooden floors today have improved the skating qualities of rinks. Numerous skate rental places have been opened, providing skates for occasional skaters who don't want to invest in their own equipment.

Also, the sudden boom in skateboards has resulted in the opening of many skateboard parks. Roller skaters are usually welcome here, too. Skateboard parks have many unusual dips, turns and circles that turn skating into real thrill rides.

In this book we have had room only for the highlights which a beginner must know. There is much more to skating, but it is all advanced work.

If you want to advance in skating, talk to the pro at a skating rink. He can point you in the right direction. Then it is just a continuation of the way you learned beginning skating. You just keep adding something new to the old that you have already learned. In this step-by-step manner, you climb right on up to the top.

Good luck to you in your pursuit of the fun of roller skating!

GLOSSARY

Apex—either of the points where the imaginary long axis line of a figure-skating set of circles crosses the top and bottom line of the set of circles.

Carrying Foot (leg or skate)—the foot or leg that supports the body's weight in skating. This continually changes from right foot to left foot, but the carrying foot, leg or skate is always the one on which your weight is riding.

Circle 8—also known as Figure 8, this is the first of the compulsory school figures in figure skating. The Circle 8 pattern is made of two circles touching at one point. The skater circles first one and then the other circle to follow an 8 track.

Cushions—these are the rubber spacers attached to the truck and a pivot point. They compress when weight is placed on the edges of the skate plate. This causes the skate track to curve. This is what makes figure skating possible. The cushions are compressed by leaning the body to either side as you skate.

Edge—an edge is a skating curve created by leaning the body to one side or the other. Edges are called outside or inside edges, depending on which side the skater leans. An inside edge is toward the open arch side of the foot. An outside edge is the opposite side.

Employed Foot (leg or skate)—this is another name for carrying foot. It is the foot, leg or skate, depending upon how the term is used, that the skater rides upon. (*See* Carrying Foot.)

Free Foot (leg or skate)—the foot that is off the ground while skating. It is also called the "Unemployed Foot." A free foot must be in the air. While pushing off, it is the "Pushing Foot."

Freestyle—this is the second portion of figure-skating competition. In freestyle a skater develops his or her own routine and is judged upon originality as well as skating ability.

Lean—the angle of the body. By leaning to one side, the skater compresses the cushions on that side, causing the skate to travel in a curved path.

Mohawk Turn—a means of reversing direction by extending the free foot backward with toe pointed in the other direction and shifting weight from the Employed Foot to the opposite foot. In this way the opposite foot becomes the Employed or Carrying Foot.

Pattern—the design to be skated in doing compulsory school figures.

Pivot—a part of the truck which permits slight movement to make leaning easier.

Plate—the flat metal base attached to the sole of the skater's shoe or boot. The opposite side of the plate holds the wheels, trucks and toestops.

Polyurethane—a type of durable plastic used to make skate wheels.

Pushing Foot—in takeoff or stroking this is the foot that provides the power for the skater to move. The pushing foot is shoved back and slightly to the side to create resistance and push the skater along. It is opposite from the carrying foot. The pushing foot becomes the Free Foot as it is rotated forward.

Rotation—moving parts of the body to aid in skating. For example, the free leg is rotated forward after a pushoff. You may also rotate your arms, hips and head on occasion.

RSROA—initials of the Roller Skating Rink Operators Association. This is an organization devoted to promoting skating. It sponsors many competition events.

School Figures—compulsory skating routines that follow definite patterns in figure-skating competitions. Compulsory school figures are skated on two-circle or three-circle patterns.

Serpentine Figure—one of the family of school figures that uses a three-circle pattern.

Skateboard—a shaped board with skate wheels attached.

Slalom—a downhill run in which the skater weaves around pylons. The term was borrowed from skiing.

Spin—to circle around a fixed point.

Toestop—a rubber bumper attached to the front of the skate plate. When the skate is tilted forward, the toestop rubs the rink or pavement to create a braking action.

Truck—the assembly that holds the wheel axle. The pivot and cushions are part of the truck assembly. There are both front and rear trucks.

Urethane—a shortened form of "polyurethane," the plastic that many skate wheels are made of.

Index

ABOUT THE AUTHOR

I. G. EDMONDS was born in Texas. He served with the Army Air Corps and the Air Force until 1963. His assignments took him all over the world, providing him with many experiences for his writing. For three years he was a feature writer for *Pacific Stars and Stripes*. During this time he traveled throughout Asia, including Thailand, Cambodia, Korea, and Japan.

He is the author of over eighty books, including *Motorcycle Racing for Beginners*, which will soon be published in an Archway edition, and *Minibikes and Minicycles for Beginners*.

Mr. Edmonds has lived in the Los Angeles area for the past fifteen years. He is married and has one daughter.